HEATWAVE, SNOW, FOG, FLOOD AND TEMPEST

HEATWAVE, SNOW, FOG, FLOOD AND TEMPEST

BY

MICHAEL KING

FINIAL PUBLISHING

First published 2005 by
FINIAL PUBLISHING LTD

ISBN 1-900467-24-X

Produced by Finial Publishing Ltd
15 Abingdon Drive, Caversham Park, Reading, Berks RG4 6SA, England
Tel/Fax: 0118-9484103
'www.finial.ndirect.co.uk'
Email: 'mail@finial.co.uk'

CONTENTS

PREFACE   vii

CHAPTER 1:   BARRAGE BALLOONS, THE BIG FREEZE   1
             AND BRILLIANT BATTING

CHAPTER 2:   EIGHTIES AT EASTER AND SEVENTIES AT SUMMER CAMP   5

CHAPTER 3:   OVERCOATS AT EASTER AND CAPES AT SUMMER CAMP   11

CHAPTER 4:   SNOW CHAOS, SQUARE BASHING AND SMOG   17

CHAPTER 5:   FLOODS, FREEZE UP AND FORKED LIGHTNING   25

CHAPTER 6:   WOMENS' QUARTERS, WARM BEER   33
             AND WRETCHED JELLYFISH

CHAPTER 7:   ON A PERSONAL (NOT A WEATHER) FRONT   41

CHAPTER 8:   SAD TIMES   47

CHAPTER 9:   A WHITE EASTER, A STORMY SEPTEMBER   51
             AND A GLORIOUS SUMMER

CHAPTER 10: RELATIVELY QUIET ON THE WEATHER FRONT,   57
             BUT A TIME OF CHANGE ON A PERSONAL FRONT

CHAPTER 11: THE WINTER OF 1962-63   63

CHAPTER 12: THE MID-SIXTIES   69

CHAPTER 13: THE IGHTHAM RAPIDS   77

CHAPTER 14: A WHITE CHRISTMAS   81

CHAPTER 15: THE SUMMER OF 1976 AND THE WINTER OF DISCONTENT   87

CHAPTER 16: ANXIOUS TIMES   93

CHAPTER 17: FAMILY HOLIDAYS AT SIDMOUTH   97

CHAPTER 18: HEAVY SNOW, HOUSE STRUCK BY LIGHTNING   103
             AND HURRICANE

CHAPTER 19: WEATHER 1988-91   109

Just before my book went to print, the world's biggest earthquake for 40 years struck 155 miles south-east of Sumatra unleashing a tsunami which caused terrible flooding in Indonesia, Sri Lanka, Thailand and other places around the Indian Ocean and as far away as the east coast of Africa. This resulted in catastrophic damage and loss of life.

My experiences of inclement weather in England between 1947 and 1991 as described in my book therefore pale into insignificance. After much deliberation I have decided to go ahead with my book only because of family and possibly historical interest.

I am humbly thankful that me and my family are safe and well and have never experienced anything like the indescribable horror which occurred in South East Asia on Boxing Day 2004.

MICHAEL KING

PREFACE

We British love to talk about the weather and when we meet somebody whom we know - and even if we don't know them - we often break the ice by commenting on how hot or cold, sunny or dull, or rainy or windy the weather is.

Being born in 1934 and at the time of writing being aged 70, the weather is a subject, which has fascinated me over the years. I do not, however, have 70 years of weather to write about. Perhaps my earliest recollection was regarding a storm around 1943, when forked lightning punctured most of the barrage balloons in the skies above South-East London, but it was the bitterly cold winter of 1947 that I recall most vividly.

The most exceptional periods of weather that I can recall are the bitterly cold winters of 1947 and 1962-63 and the month of January 1979, during the so-called 'winter of discontent'.

I also recall in the following pages, the gorgeous summers of 1947, 1955, 1959, 1975, 1983, 1984, 1989 and 1990, but not forgetting the best one of all, the summer of 1976.

Less happy memories recall the dreadful smog, which enveloped London between 5-9th December 1952, and the thick fog on the night of December 4th 1957, which caused the horrendous Lewisham train crash. I also write about the East Coast floods which occurred at the end of January 1953 and the floods in September 1968,when large parts of South London and Kent were flooded.

The year which I remember most with regard to the weather, is however 1987, the depth of the snow in the middle of January, the like of which I had neither seen, nor seen since. The same year, our house was struck by lightning on 21st August and, of course, the Great Hurricane, which occurred on the night of 15th-16th October and I write in some detail about these events.

I also make a brief mention here of the mini-hurricane, which occurred during the daytime in January 1990 and which, surprisingly, did more damage to our property than the Great Hurricane of 1987. I also write about the record temperatures experienced at the beginning of August that year.

Although I regard the above as the most exceptional climatic events that I have experienced, I have written also about other quite remarkable weather.

I have recounted quite a number of personal experiences, some of which I hope the reader may find interesting, as although the book is principally about the weather, I have also given a brief account of my life in general from January 1947, to the date of my retirement from the bank where I worked, on 31st December 1991.

I have decided to end my book at this point and I hope that I have managed to put together a book, which is reasonably interesting. However, because of the 'mists of time', it is quite probable that I have forgotten some other instances of exceptional weather and for that, I hope that the reader will forgive me.

MICHAEL KING

Alleyns School, Winter 1947.

Chapter One

BARRAGE BALLOONS, THE BIG FREEZE AND BRILLIANT BATTING

I was born in 1934, but the first exceptional weather that I can remember was the long and bitterly cold winter of 1947. I cannot really remember what the previous weather was like at all, except for one afternoon around 1943, when I was returning home from school.

I attended a small private school by the name of South Hill College in Mayow Road, Sydenham and that day, as usual, Miss Cowley, the Principal let us leave at 3 p.m. It was about a mile walk to my home and as I was walking down the Sydenham Road, it started to rain. By the time I reached Bell Green, the sky had turned really dark. Then suddenly,

1

lightning flashed, followed by loud peals of thunder. It also started to rain heavily. With that, I raced down Southend Lane and sought sanctuary in a telephone kiosk, located at the front of a row of shops.

What I was about to see would amaze me. Barrage balloons were up in the sky. The balloons were designed to prevent German aircraft from flying too low over London. The thunder and lightning grew worse and suddenly, I saw that the balloons were starting to disintegrate, punctured by the forked lightning. By the time that the storm had abated, there were hardly any balloons left in the sky.

On the night of January 23rd 1947, snow fell on the South East of England and I believe in most other parts of Britain. The next morning I awoke to a pretty Christmas card scene, 'Good', I thought, 'This weekend I can go tobogganing on an old piece of Anderson shelter on the slopes of some waste ground just off Southend Lane and take part in some snowball fights'. But, it started snowing later on that day and went on snowing all over the weekend, the snow being driven by some bitterly cold East winds. It was even worse the following week. The snow was so deep and the weather so bitterly cold, that I abandoned all thoughts of snowball fights and tobogganing and tried to keep warm indoors. In any case, I'm sure that my parents would not have let me go in such conditions.

After that awful weekend, I managed to get to school, but I had to walk the three miles or so from Forest Hill to East Dulwich, as the tram tracks were filled with ice and the points were frozen. At least during that time, I did not have to worry about being late for school and having my name taken at the gate by a school prefect. My form mistress - Miss Wiggs - who could be a real dragon, was really understanding and let us thaw out in front of the big stove in the classroom, before getting down to lessons.

But soon, fuel was to be a problem. The boats, which supplied coal to London, were frozen up in the northern ports and road and rail services were heavily disrupted by the snow. Many main roads were impassable and snowdrifts of up to 10-feet deep were reported.

It was a good job that the school had a good supply of old, unusable furniture. This furniture was chopped up and the stoves and fires kept going by using wood. I recall that, thankfully, coal was delivered to the school just in time, as I think that the school was probably down to its last chair-leg!

Snow fell every day from 23rd January until 15th March during that awful winter. Strangely enough, I do not really remember what life was like at home during that time. We had a large coal cellar and I think we must have had a big delivery just before the Big Freeze, as I don't remember feeling really cold at home. We had a very snug little kitchen. We certainly wouldn't have used the front room, which was freezing at the best of times, during the Big Freeze and although I cannot now remember, we would have probably had extra blankets on the bed and two or three hot water bottles.

On 1st March, I went with my Dad and Uncle Henry to see a 6th Round FA Cup-Tie between Charlton Athletic, whom I supported, and Preston North End. We found ourselves standing in about six-inches of frozen slush on the terraces at the Valley. It turned out to be an exciting cup-tie and what with the brilliance of Tom Finney, we soon forgot about our frozen feet. Their captain, the great Bill Shankly, also had an outstanding game and I shall never forget the look of sheer determination on his face during that match. But, in spite of their best efforts, Charlton won the match 2-1 with a hotly disputed goal. Charlton went on to win the FA Cup that year, beating Second Division Burnley by one goal to nil (after extra time).

That year, the weather so disrupted the Football League programme, that I actually watched a match between Millwall and Burnley at the beginning of June!

The awful winter was, however, followed by a glorious summer. We had marvellous weather day after day, but Tom, our Sunday School teacher would have to choose the one really bad day in June for our annual outing.

That day, we walked to Beckenham Hill station to catch a train to Shoreham, a pretty little village in Kent, not far from Sevenoaks. Unfortunately, by the time we arrived at Shoreham station, it had started to rain torrentially and so it continued all day long until we arrived home. There was nothing that we could really do except tramp through the woods around Shoreham in the rain. I remember that we ate our soggy sandwiches underneath a deserted bandstand in Shoreham. Tom could see that we were so disappointed and promised another outing later in the summer.

During the half-term holiday, I went on a hazardous adventure (for a 13-year-old boy!). I caught a number 108 bus to the Crystal Palace and then caught a number 2 bus from there to Lords Cricket Ground. Middlesex were playing Yorkshire and I went along in the hope of seeing the 'Terrible Twins' Bill Edrich and Denis Compton in action. It was a beautiful day and also the first day of a County match between Middlesex and Yorkshire. I was, therefore, delighted when I saw the Yorkshire players taking the field. However, I had to wait a long time before I could see my heroes bat. The two openers - Robertson and

Brown - scored 108 and 130 runs respectively. I then saw a feast of batting from Edrich and Compton, but when the former had scored 54 not out and the latter 50 not out, the Middlesex captain declared.

When it was Yorkshire's turn to bat, wickets began to fall rapidly, except for that of the great Len Hutton who was undefeated at the close of play.

Compton and Edrich each scored over 3,000 runs during that glorious summer. Compton scored a record 3816 runs in a season; a record that I think is unlikely to be surpassed. I had felt very grown-up and independent having made the journey to Lords and this gave me the confidence to make more bus and train journeys of reasonable length. I finished a most enjoyable day by having a lemonade and a bite to eat at a cafe on Crystal Palace Parade on the way home.

On August Bank Holiday Monday, Tom took the Sunday School on another outing to make up for the miserable time that we had had in June. This time the weather was glorious. We caught a train from Beckenham Hill station to Sevenoaks, where we caught another train to Tunbridge Wells. We then walked the four miles or so to the village of Penshurst. We then went to Penshurst church were Tom's father was the vicar and his brother the curate. They showed us around the church and then provided us with a nice meal which, I think was taken in the Church Hall.

We had a lovely day in Penshurst, but all too soon, it was time to leave. Tom decided that we walk the short distance to Penshurst station and then catch a train to Tonbridge. By the time we arrived, the heat had made us feel pretty thirsty, so we all went into the station buffet to partake in a refreshing glass of lemonade. There we found some Bank Holiday revellers, who were obviously on something stronger than lemonade, singing with gusto, the 1947 hit 'Near You'. I arrived home tired, but happy after a lovely day in perfect weather.

It really had been a glorious summer, but the following one was disappointing by comparison and as I have no particular memories of 1948 as regards to the weather, I am going to move on to 1949.

A picture of the author taken on Charmouth beach
during the glorious weather in August.

Chapter Two

EIGHTIES AT EASTER AND SEVENTIES AT SUMMER CAMP

I joined the 2nd Sydenham (St. Michael's) Scout Troop in February 1948, a month after it had re-opened after the war. We just had one camp that year, a weekend camp in July, held at Frylands Woods, Addington, Surrey and as I recall this, this weekend was fine without being really hot.

The next camp that I attended was at Easter 1949, held again at Frylands Woods. It was my birthday on the Easter Monday and I tried to keep this fact dark from my Scouters and fellow Scouts, because normally, on one's birthday, on the Thursday night Troop meeting nearest to one's birthday, one would just have to put up with being 'bumped' (the number of bumps being commensurate with one's age, plus about three 'for luck'). However, if you were unfortunate enough to have your birthday at camp, you would get covered in blacking, mixed with toothpaste. Because of this, I aimed to leave camp first thing on the Monday morning. But first, I had to find a good excuse!

So, I asked Gran if she would like to come with me on an outing to Shoreham in Kent. After she said, "Yes, I would like to", I craftily asked Albert, our Skipper, if I could leave camp early, as I wanted to take Gran out in the afternoon. Needless to say, I made no mention that Mum and Dad were coming as well. Permission was granted.

The weather during that week was sensational and the temperature during the day was in the eighties throughout, a record Easter temperature being recorded at Camden, in London on Saturday 16th April. That afternoon, we went down to the field on the fringe of the camp to have a game of football, but it was so hot, that we soon stopped playing and laid on the grass to sunbathe.

On the other side of Featherbed Lane, which ran alongside the camp, were some steep hills and some riders were putting their horses through their paces in the blazing heat. This sight particularly angered Tim, the Cub Leader, who remarked, "I would like to jump on the backs of those riders and ride them up those hills in this heat and see how they would like it".

The weather was glorious also on Easter Sunday. We had an open-air Church Service in the morning and we were thankful that the open-air Chapel was sheltered by trees. In fact about 90% of Frylands Woods is wooded and we were certainly thankful for that during the exceptional Easter heat.

Monday duly came round. It was a glorious morning again and I got up and walked out of my tent and looked around me. Everything looked perfectly normal with people getting on with their chores and I thought to myself, 'I do believe that everybody has forgotten that it's my Birthday today'. With that thought, I went back into the tent, rolled up my bedding and put it, together with my other kit into my rucksack, leaving just my washing gear and my Scout uniform out. I washed and then went to breakfast, which the Duty Patrol had cooked.

When breakfast was finished, I went up to Albert and asked him, could I put on my uniform, in order to leave camp? "Not so fast, Michael", he said. "We have not given you your Birthday present yet". 'Who could have grassed me up?' I thought. Then suddenly, the penny dropped. My cousin Michael was also at camp, in one of the other patrols and he, of

6

course, would have known the date of my birthday. So, I duly received my 'birthday present' and I had to go back to the washhouse, this time using a scrubbing brush to get the mixture of blacking and toothpaste off.

Then, at last, I was able to leave camp and I walked up the steep hill to the village of New Addington with my back to the blazing heat. 'Now I know how those horses must have felt', I thought. I caught a number 130 bus from the terminus there, got off at Shirley and then caught a number 194, which took me home, arriving there at about lunchtime.

I knocked on door with some anticipation, after all, it was my birthday and I was hoping for some cards and presents. I was not disappointed, with cards and presents from Mum and Dad, my brother Geoff, my two grandmothers and from other friends and relations.

After lunch, Mum, Dad, Gran and I walked to Beckenham Hill station in order to catch a train to Shoreham. It was a glorious afternoon and we walked from Shoreham station to the lovely 'olde worlde' village, where we ate a lovely cream tea. Then we walked some way along the River Darenth and I reflected that Shoreham in the glorious Easter sunshine looked totally different to the rainswept place that we had visited on our Sunday School outing two years previously. I felt tired, but happy, when I arrived home, after all the walking and travelling in the heat, but it had been a glorious day and a super birthday (apart from my 'birthday present' at camp!).

A very good summer followed that fantastic Easter. The Troop were going on their first Summer Camp since the war, Albert getting in touch with a farmer in Charmouth, West Dorset, inquiring whether the Troop could camp on his land for a fortnight in August. Albert probably already knew the farmer, as the pre-war Troop used to spend their summer camps at Charmouth or on a farm at Eype, near Bridport. Anyway, permission was soon forthcoming.

It was a boiling hot day when we all walked to Lower Sydenham station, to catch a train to Waterloo carrying our heavy rucksacks. "I don't know how hot it is going to get, but it's a stinker already!", I heard Albert say to Ron.

We alighted from the train at Waterloo East, then walked along a passageway which led to the main station. We then walked across the station concourse to one of the platforms, where a board announced that the train was stopping at Basingstoke, Salisbury, Yeovil, and Axminster, before terminating at Exeter Central. The loudspeaker further announced that one had to change at Axminster for Lyme Regis. We boarded the train at Waterloo and Albert's father saw us off. He was an enormous man, who had been a policeman, keeping law and order in Sydenham.

Dad used to say that no one dared cross him, but I found him a quite a pleasant man. Albert's father's parting words were, *"You mind you all behave!"*.

In due course we reached Axminster, alighted from the train and walked across the platform and boarded a quaint little 'Puffing Billy'. The train was to take us the relatively short distance to Lyme Regis, stopping at a little station named Combpyne. When we alighted from the train at Lyme, my gaze was arrested by a stunning view across Lyme Bay.

Albert had brought with him on the train, his cycle and trailer, which packed with lightweight camping gear, the main camping gear having been sent on in advance to the farmer. He was to use the trailer to collect provisions from the village while we were at camp. Tim had also brought his bike with him and they both set off towards Charmouth, although I did not envy their having to climb the long 1:7 hill between Lyme Regis and Charmouth. With that, Ron, the Assistant Skipper, marched us off to the nearest bus stop, a bus soon arriving. We were pleased to find that the bus stopped a stone's throw from the farm where we were to camp.

Once we arrived at the camp, we were all put to work. Firstly we helped Ron, Albert and Tim collect the camping gear from the farmer, then we all busied ourselves putting up tents, digging latrines etc. Albert had designated one patrol as the duty patrol and they had to get water from the farmhouse and carry it back in large 'dixies' (a dixie was a large cooking utensil). The patrol then had to collect wood, get a fire going and cook the Troop an evening meal.

The duty patrol provided us with a good meal as I recall and afterwards we had to organise our own personal belongings and do odd jobs round the camp. We went to bed feeling worn out by a very active day in the blazing heat.

The day we arrived at camp, the temperature must have been in the eighties but thankfully after that it dropped a little and the day-time temperature for the rest of the fortnight hovered around the mid-seventies. It was perfect weather for swimming and we went to the beach every afternoon, except for the two Thursdays which were the traditional days off for the Scouts and the Scouters and where we could do anything we liked, within reason The rule about swimming without a Scouter present was, quite rightly strictly enforced, so, therefore, we did not swim on those days. Charmouth possessed a lovely sandy beach in beautiful surroundings, under the shadow of Golden Cap, the highest point on the Dorset coast,

Mornings, apart from Thursdays, were spent in camp where the boys practised Scoutcraft, such as tree and bird recognition, the estimation of distances, semaphore, knots and lashings etc and as previously mentioned, the afternoons were spent swimming in idyllic weather off Charmouth.

I became very fond of Lyme Regis as well, with its lovely sands and its 'Cobb' - made famous in the film 'The French Lieutenant's Woman` - its steep streets, quaint shops and above all, for the breathtaking scenery in and around the town.

All too soon it was time to return home. We travelled back using the same route and when we eventually arrived at Lower Sydenham station, I was lucky, as I had less than a five-minute walk to my home. Naturally, I was very pleased about this, as my rucksack was pretty heavy.

It had been a great summer camp in lovely weather, but the next year was going to produce some really miserable weather.

Picture of the Scout Troop taken at Summer Camp 1950 on Charmouth beach.
Most of us are covered up against the chill wind.

Chapter Three

OVERCOATS AT EASTER AND CAPES AT SUMMER CAMP

Easter Camp in 1950 was again held at Frylands Woods. The weather was miserable throughout and there was a bitterly cold wind blowing all the time. I was just thankful that Frylands was a wooded camp and that we were not camping in open fields, as the wind chill would have seemed much worse. How I longed for the gorgeous weather of the previous Easter. Instead of sunbathing and wearing only shorts, we spent almost the entire time wearing pullovers and windcheaters. When Mum and Dad came to visit me at camp on the Easter Sunday they were both wearing overcoats. It was a most forgettable camp and, therefore, I do not have much to say about it.

Summer Camp was again held at Charmouth. We camped at the same farm, but in a different field. This time we did not have to travel down by train, as Albert had hired a pantechnicon to take the boys and the camping gear down to Charmouth. Since the previous Summer Camp, Albert had acquired a motor car - an Austin 7 - and he drove down in the car accompanied by a Rover Scout, who was a St. Michael's 'Old Boy' by the name of Ivor. He used to help out at Troop Meetings occasionally, but we had not seen much of him, as he spent most of his time in West Africa. I think that he worked for a pharmaceutical company out there. He was on leave at the time we were going to camp, so he asked Albert if he could come with us. There were, therefore, three Scouters attending this camp, as well as the previous one, with Ivor replacing Tim. Tim had taken up a Commission in the Merchant Navy and had resigned as Cub Leader a week after the previous Summer Camp. A young lady by the name of Margaret had taken over as Akela.

The boys all travelled down in the back of the pantechnicon, with Ron D in charge of us. It was a fairly nice day without being unbearably hot. The driver stopped on the way down so that we could have some refreshments. I don't remember exactly where we stopped, but it was a pleasant enough cafe, as I recall, with a juke-box playing Bing Crosby's 'Home Cooking' on our arrival. It's amazing how some little things stick in your mind about a place or an event when all other memories of it have gone.

I recall that the lorry arrived at the camp about the same time as Ron and Ivor and we all pitched in with the work in setting up camp.

The weather during the first week was generally cold and miserable, with one or two sunny spells in between. We went swimming two or three times that week, but I did not stay in the water long, because it was so cold.

On our first free Thursday off, the Scouters and the boys caught a bus to Bridport, a market town situated about eight miles away from Charmouth. From there, they intended to walk a distance of about 1.5 miles to the seaside village of West Bay. My cousin Michael and I, however - mad fools that we were - decided to walk to Bridport and then on to West Bay, a distance of around 10 miles, where we would meet the rest of the Troop. I don't know why we walked all that way, but perhaps it was to prove that we could. But we were certainly glad to get on the bus for the journey back to Charmouth.

We were all affected by the general cold and dampness, but no one suffered more than Ivor, who had just returned to this country from the

12

heat of West Africa. Albert and Ron each lent him an extra blanket, but still he was cold which, unsurprisingly, made him rather grumpy at times.

If the weather during the first week was cold and miserable, it was appalling during most of the second.

The torrential rain started to fall about mid-morning on the second Monday. The duty patrol had kept the fire going since breakfast, in order that it would be nice and hot by the time they had to cook lunch. The duty patrol started to prepare lunch, but it soon became impossible in the driving rain and in about half an hour, it had put out the fire. The boys managed to relight it, but in no time at all, the rain had extinguished it again; this happened one more time, then Albert said, "Enough of this, you boys will all go back into your tents; Ron, Ivor and I will rig up a shelter, put up a trestle-table underneath it, and cook your lunch on Primus stoves". So, the Scouters made a shelter out of some old groundsheets and tent poles, put up a table and started to cook our lunch, which they served us in our tents. In order to provide some protection from the driving rain, the Scouters donned their wide-brimmed hats and capes. The weather was so bad that this procedure was repeated on the next two days.

The culmination of this appalling weather was a storm, which took place around dawn on the Thursday morning. *The rain had completely washed out the three bell-tents in which the three Patrols slept.* By some miracle, the ridge-tent in which I was sleeping with my fellow Senior Scouts had escaped the floods; likewise the Scouters' ridge-tent had also not been affected. I remember that my aunt had bought Michael a brand new white sleeping bag just before this camp, but this was no longer pristine white, as mud had also swept into the tent.

As explained earlier, Thursday was our traditional day off when we could do as we liked, apart from going swimming unsupervised. By breakfast time, the rain had stopped and Albert decided that he wanted the boys off the camp, so that he, Ron and Ivor could start drying out the boys' bedding. The Scouters would, therefore, forego their day off in order to get the job done. There was, however, one condition and that was we were only allowed to go to nearby Lyme Regis, a distance of around two miles. The reason for that decision was that if any Scout became lost, the Scouters did not want to have to travel miles to try to find him.

Once we were all off the camp, the Scouters made huge frames from dead branches of trees which they found, the branches being lashed together with rope. They then hung the boys' bedding over these frames in front of the fire to dry. Apparently this task required constant supervision in case any of the bedding got singed or burnt, thus adding

13

to the problems that they already faced.

I again spent our free day with my cousin Michael and when we, arrived at Lyme Regis, we decided that it was too cold and miserable to spend the day on the beach, so we spent it in the Regent cinema watching a film titled, appropriately enough 'Neptune's Daughter', starring former swimming champion Esther Williams and Ricardo Montalban. We saw plenty of water in the film too! I enjoyed the film, however, because even at that early age, I loved Latin American music. This was provided by the band of Xavier Cugat, probably the best exponents of Latin-American music that I have listened to.

When we returned to camp, Albert announced to the boys that their bedding was completely dry. As I recall the weather then remained fine and dry until the end of camp. However, I do remember that we were later than usual leaving camp on the Saturday, as it was getting dark and the street lights were on as the lorry drove through Sutton and parts of Croydon.

In due course the lorry arrived back at the Church Hall and I was only too glad to get off the lorry and forget about this miserable Summer Camp. That was, until Mum handed me an envelope containing my miserable School Certificate results. I discovered that I had gained a distinction in French (thanks to Miss Wiggs!) but only passes in English Grammar and German. I have written about Miss Wiggs in my previous book 'Recollections of the 1950s'. I was in the 5th term at Alleyns School, the year prior to taking my School Certificate and in Miss Wiggs class of 19 pupils, there were 12 distinctions and six cedits, an achievement reported in a national newspaper.

I will conclude this chapter by writing about the only really hot weather that I can remember in 1950, which was a weekend in July. Albert decided to take us on a weekend camp at Downe, a village situated near Orpington in Kent. This was an Official Scout Association campsite, as was Frylands Woods. I recall that the site was run by a distinguished-looking man by the name of Major Seager. Generally speaking, I did not like this site as much as Frylands Woods, as it seemed very open after the treesheltered Frylands. But, Downe had one big advantage that blazing hot weekend. It possessed an open-air swimming pool!

When we had finished setting up camp in the blazing heat, we all thankfully plunged into the pool. The pool was unheated but we scarcely noticed that. Albert then detailed some lads to prepare tea, while the rest of us did other chores around the site. In the evening there was a camp-fire, after which we all went to bed tired after an active day.

The following day was even hotter. We attended an open air Church

Service and I was stood with my back to the boiling sun. The back of my neck seemed to be getting hotter and hotter, until suddenly I felt faint and then passed out and I could vaguely sense being dragged into the shade. Soon, I came to, but found myself lying in a bed of nettles. Needless to say, I did not lay there long.

Some of the boys then cooked a midday meal, but after lunch it became unbearably humid. Suddenly there were flashes of lightning, followed by loud peals of thunder. It also started to rain torrentially and Albert told us to go into our tents. Then things began to get really scary; the lightning crackled and the thunder roared. Suddenly, the burly figure of Albert appeared at the door of the tent. "How are you all?", he asked.

"Scared!", we all replied.

"There's no point in worrying", he said, "if a bolt of lightning has got your number on it, there's nothing you can do about it".

This may have sounded insensitive, but in fact, Albert was one of the most caring persons I have come across. He looked - and was - as tough as old boots and I daresay the thunder and lightning had not scared him, as he had been a Chief Petty Officer in the Royal Navy during the war and had had to contend with the ever-present threat of U-boats, torpedoes and planes. Soon after that the storm abated and we started to strike camp before returning home.

I have few memories of the weather during 1951, but in March I left school and started work in a bank in April. I cannot remember any heatwaves, but I recall that the weather was generally pleasant during the summer. I used to travel between Charing Cross and Waterloo East on my way home from work on the evenings. The train used to go through the South Bank site of the Festival of Britain and I would look down from the train to see everyone enjoying the attractions there.

The duration of Summer Camp that year was a week, instead of a fortnight and by some miracle, I managed to get this week in August as leave. It was usually impossible for the junior clerk to get a holiday anywhere near August, but there was a spare week going which the more senior staff did not want as their main holiday. There was only one problem, however, I had to work on the Saturday morning. Alternatively, one had to prove to the bank manager that you were travelling more than 200 miles to one's holiday destination and Arundel - our camp venue for that year - was hardly 200 miles away from London!

Albert and Ron were travelling in Albert's Austin 7 and the boys and the camping gear were following in a lorry. However, as I did not arrive home from work until nearly 2 p.m., after quick bite to eat, I then caught a bus to Sydenham station, where I purchased a return ticket to Arundel, having to change at West Croydon.

Unfortunately, the weather was appalling that Saturday and when I arrived at the site, I found that everyone was saturated after the efforts of pitching camp in the driving rain. By the time I arrived, the work had been done and my mates were somewhat grumpy, which I could well understand under the circumstances, although it was hardly my fault that I had to work in the morning. After a good night's sleep, however, all was forgotten and we had a very good week in pleasant weather, which was not too hot. Albert used to ferry the boys in his Austin 7 between camp and Clymping beach most days. We played football and cricket on camp, explored the lovely Sussex countryside around Arundel and visited Arundel and Littlehampton.

As mentioned previously, I cannot remember too much about the weather in 1951, so I will now move on to the following year.

Picture of my Intake at The Royal Army Pay Corps Training Centre, Devizes, taken on a blazing hot day in August 1952.

Chapter Four

SNOW CHAOS, SQUARE BASHING AND SMOG

My first memory of 1952 was hearing the sad news of the death of King George VIth on 6th February. There was a genuine feeling of grief among the people, as they remembered the sense of duty the King and Queen Elizabeth showed when the King refused offers to take himself and his family to the safety of Canada during the war. The Royal Family stayed at Buckingham Palace to face the Blitz in 1940, the King and the Queen visiting people in the East End of London and in other parts of the country who had been bombed out of their homes.

This was why there was such a massive crowd in the Edgware Road where I worked at that time and along all other parts of the funeral route, as the King had been a much-loved and respected Monarch. The funeral procession was scheduled to go up the Edgware Road towards Paddington Station, where his coffin would be put on the Royal Train. From there, the coffin would be taken to Windsor where the King would be buried.

I worked in a bank in the Edgware Road and the manager had been instructed by Head Office not to open the branch until after the procession had passed by and the vast crowds had dispersed. Travelling to work was a problem on that day - Friday 15th February - and I could not get to work from Charing Cross by bus, as the Edgware Road had been completely closed to traffic. It would have been impossible to have got a tube to Marble Arch Station, as there was no way I could have fought my way to work through the crowds. So, I decided to catch a Bakerloo Line train to Paddington, where I met up with three other colleagues from the bank. We then made our way through the side streets and let ourselves in through the side door of the bank.

It had been a bleak, raw, cold morning and this seemed to add to the solemnity of the occasion. When I arrived at the branch, I noticed that the manager was already there. On seeing me, he said, "Mr. King. I want you to completely cover the counter with brown paper, so when we hear the procession approaching, we can all stand on the counter and get a good view of it. I have also asked a few customers, so I want you to supply them with tea or coffee and biscuits when they arrive". In those days, the banks had completely open counters.

I stood on the counter when I had finished my handiwork with the brown paper and looked out into the Edgware Road. Genuine grief was etched on the faces of the spectators and in front of them, stood the Guardsmen, stiff as ramrods, with their rifles at "The Reverse Slope" in mourning, which conveyed a feeling of great solemnity.

The customers duly arrived and received their tea coffee and biscuits, after which I went downstairs to wash up the cups, saucers etc. Our branch was too small to be entitled to the services of a messenger, so the office junior had to do a lot of menial jobs.

When I returned upstairs, there was suddenly a flurry of action and I could hear in the distance, the strains of Beethoven's "Funeral March". Staff and customers then took up their positions on the counter. Suddenly, the front of the procession came into view and we watched this solemn procession, until when the gun-carriage passed bearing the King's coffin, the feeling of grief was almost tangible.

Once the procession had passed by and the crowd had dispersed, the manager's 'pet' customers then left. Shortly afterwards, the manager opened the branch. The time must have been around mid-day and usually on Friday afternoons, the branch was packed with customers, but we had very few customers that afternoon, as few people had the spirit to do any banking transactions and so we all went home around 4 p.m.

On Friday 7th March, I went with my father to Olympia to see the Ideal Home Exhibition. I used to go every year, as Dad received free tickets for this event. He was the Chief Stores Officer at the Sydenham Gas Company and, as such, used to have a lot of contact with the reps. of the large gas cooker companies, such as Parkinson Cowan, New World etc. who would send him free tickets for the Exhibition. Dad also gave me some tickets to give to some of my colleagues in the bank. I really enjoyed going to this event, as we would visit the reps in their little offices on their stands, alcohol would flow liberally and I was allowed a glass or two. I remember wondering that if the reps drank all day like this, how did they ever manage to get any work done?

Eventually, we left the Exhibition and headed for Olympia Tube station. We had to get to Charing Cross Railway station, although I cannot remember now whether we had to change? At Charing Cross, we got in a train going to Hayes, which stopped at Lower Sydenham. There, we alighted from the train and walked over the footbridge. It was then that I noticed how cold it had become. There was a bitterly north-east wind blowing. As my father and I walked down the narrow alleyway between the railway lines and the Britannic Sports Ground, the bitter north-east seemed to be racing up the alleyway and blowing into our faces. I remember hoping that Mum did not still have any washing on the line, as by now the washing would be covered in black smuts emanating from the retort houses of the Gas Works, as was always the case when a fierce north-easterly was blowing. We soon arrived home, however and warmed ourselves up in front of the fire.

It was still very cold the next morning, but, so far, no snow had fallen. I had to work on Saturday mornings, so I walked up the alleyway to Lower Sydenham station to catch my usual 8 a.m. train. When I arrived at work, I was having a quick chat with a friend by the name of John, when suddenly he said, "Look, Michael, at the amount of snow on some of the cars travelling towards Marble Arch". In those days, the Edgware Road was part of the A5, being one of the main routes to and from the North. The cars, travelling southwards, had obviously travelled some distance, with about a foot of snow on their bonnets. About 10 minutes later, the blizzard struck. You could hardly see outside for snow. The blizzard continued for most of the morning. Still, it kept most of the customers away! We had a quiet morning and I think that the snow had stopped falling by the time that I left at around 12.30 p.m. Fortunately, the continual daytime London traffic had kept the main routes open and I was able to get a bus to Charing Cross. When I arrived there, the snow had completely disrupted the timetable, but fortunately there was a Mid-Kent Line train to Hayes standing on one of the platforms, which stopped at Lower Sydenham. Soon, the train departed and I do not recall any undue delay on the journey home. But, my travelling experience on the trains in the afternoon was to be very different.

About three weeks previously, I had gone to Regos in Lewisham to get myself measured up for a suit (in those days it was usual to buy made-to-measure suits). Now it was time for me to collect it. So, at around 2 p.m., I set off for Lower Sydenham station and there I bought a return ticket to Lewisham. I knew that the heavy snow in the morning had seriously disrupted the timetable and that I would have to be careful, as not all trains stopped at Lewisham. I walked on to the platform and saw that there was a train approaching. A porter was standing on the platform, so I asked him, "Does this train stop at Lewisham?".

"Yes, mate", he replied.

I got on the train, which stopped at Catford Bridge and then Ladywell and then, to my horror, it branched off towards St. John's, before it reached Lewisham. It did not stop at St, John's Station, but it did at the next one - New Cross. Disgruntled, I walked over the bridge to the Up platform. A train approached. Again I asked a porter, "Does this train stop at Lewisham?".

"Yes", he answered.

I got on the train. It stopped at St. John's, then, to my chagrin it branched off towards Hither Green. There, I got off and walked over to the Up platform. Again, a train approached and again I asked a porter, "Does this train stop at Lewisham?".

"Yes", he said, so I got on the train.

'That's good', I thought to myself, 'Surely nothing can go wrong as Lewisham was the next stop'. To my utter disbelief, the train bypassed Lewisham and stopped at St. John's. Utterly exasperated by now, I walked over to the Down platform. Again a train approached and again I asked a porter, "Does this train stop at Lewisham?".

"Yes", he said. *And this time it actually did.*

I sped out of the station and walked to Regos where I collected my suit. I might add that I did not make use of the return half of my ticket, but walked across the road to catch a number 108 bus back to Lower Sydenham!

Opposite is a map, which helps to illustrate my trials and tribulations that afternoon.

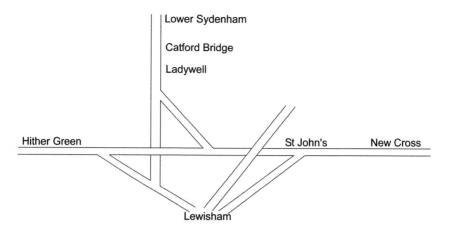

Lower Sydenham

Catford Bridge

Ladywell

Hither Green

St John's

New Cross

Lewisham

On Thursday 19th June, I had to report to the Royal Army Pay Corps Training Centre at Devizes to commence my National Service. It was a very hot day and I had to catch a train from Paddington to Patney & Chirton station in Wiltshire, from where I caught another train to Devizes. A soldier who introduced himself as a Corporal Ace met us at the station. He told us all to climb aboard the lorry, then he pulled down the tarpaulin at the back and we found it quite disorientating travelling along in virtual darkness. Fortunately, the journey from the station to the camp was a short one.

After being documented and kitted out, it was time to meet our charming NCOs! From then on, that day, they were shouting at us all the time. However, I came to respect them in the end and I discovered that there were far worse NCOs on the camp. In fact, I began to respect my Sergeant on the first night, when, during a pep talk before we went to bed, he said he would not tolerate swearing in his presence, although most of the chaps swore like troupers out of it! Although it was a very hot day, we didn't have time to think about the heat, or, in fact, anything else as we tried not to displease our NCOs too much.

The very hot weather was to continue without a break for seven weeks, with temperatures into the eighties. Drill was very tiring in the blazing hot weather, with some lads in the Platoon fainting and only the lightning reactions of our Sergeant, who was a Martial Arts expert, that stopped them hitting the ground.

Heat, unless it is really exceptional, does not affect me, although I did faint during a Open-air Scout Camp Church Service (see previous chapter), when a boiling sun was on the back of my neck all the time. I am far more likely to faint because of the cold, which I did at my next

21

camp in January, when we had been stood to attention for a long time, waiting for a General to arrive to inspect us.

The heat did, however, affect us. A lot of the lads got blisters on their feet, although fortunately, I didn't. We noticed that our Lance Corporal used to return to the hut, ashen-faced after a gruelling drill session or a fast march of about $2^1/2$ miles duration. It did not seem to affect our Sergeant, however, who was a very fit man and as tough as old boots. Our Corporal was also very fit. But one day, even our Sergeant conceded to the weather.

We had a drill period that day at 14.00 hours, immediately after lunch. The temperature must have been somewhere around 90 degrees and after the Sergeant had marched us the short distance from our barrack rooms to A Company square, he then said to us, "I want you lads to really put your backs into it for 10 minutes, as I have no intention of keeping you out any longer in this heat". Then, true to his word, he marched us back to the barrack room and let us relax on our beds.

Obviously we felt the heat during drill periods and also if we had to do PT outside the gym. Once we had a cross country run; the Corporal Gym Instructor, who was a real wide boy with only six weeks to do, told us to take a circular route and that he would follow a little way behind. When we all returned to camp, absolutely knackered in the blazing heat, he was found at one of the camp entrances, sitting on a five bar gate. "Had a good run, boys?", he asked. He, of course, had never left the camp.

One day I was struggling with the high-jump in the heat, the Corporal obviously not thinking much of my efforts, saying sarcastically, "I could pole-vault that on my prick!".

During the first seven weeks, we had to do two 'five-mile bashes' - one, in PT kit, the other, in full battle order; large pack, small pack, rifle etc. One had to walk five miles in an hour around the pretty villages near Devizes. One lad, a friend of mine, by the name of Roy Small collapsed on the first 'bash' and had to be rushed to the MI room by Army Ambulance. He was found to be asthmatic and goodness knows how he was passed fit for the Army in the first place! He was obviously excused the second 'bash' , wearing boots and all marching and PT and I think that the CSM found him various jobs for him to do around the camp.

The first wet day came after exactly seven weeks in the Training Centre. It was the dreaded 7-week inspection, which was to take place under the eagle eyes of the Adjutant and the RSM, with the Adjutant in overall charge. When it was time to leave our barrack rooms and to be marched to the square, it was pouring with rain, so we had to don our capes. Because of the weather, the Adjutant decided to hold the inspection in a drill shed adjacent to the square. Once there, he told us to discard our capes and then the inspection began. I had never known a more strict inspection. He found practically everything wrong with everybody. He told me to report to the Regimental Tailor with my best uniform in order that alterations could be made before the forthcoming Passing Out Parade, which was scheduled for Thursday August 21st. We should have had ten weeks training, but we had to get 'up to speed' in nine, as the Inspecting Officer, the Paymaster-in-Chief of the US Army could not make it on the 28th.

After the rainy 7-week Inspection, the weather remained fine for the next two weeks, but thankfully, not so hot. Also, we no longer had to do PT and Weapon Training, but in the mornings, had to undergo Clerical Tests, so that the powers-that-be could assess our suitability for work in a Pay Office. In the afternoons, we had rehearsals for the Passing Out Parade under the eagle-eye of CSM Offer.

At last the big day arrived and firstly we had a rigorous inspection in the morning by the CSM. Some lads were told to shave again and some rushed to the Camp Barbers for another haircut. After that we sat in our barracks feeling nervous. At one point, the CSM came in and said, "Don't worry about some gum-chewing Yank, you'll be alright".

The US Brigadier General was due to arrive at 12 noon, so we were paraded again at 11.30 hrs. An Orderly came with us, carrying a duster in case a soldier had got a speck or two of dust on his boots while marching to the square. For the next half hour, we tried to relax, then at 12.00 hours sharp, we received the order "*G-e-n-e-r-a-l S-a-l-u-t-e, Present Arms!*". At that point, two Staff Cars drove on to the square, one carrying the US Brigadier General and Major-General Bednall, our Paymaster-in-Chief; the second car bore the Commandant, Colonel Malpass and the Adjutant, Captain Shaw. The Company Commander saluted the Senior Officers and then the inspection commenced.

I have never come across a 'Brass hat' less stuffy as the US Brigadier-General. To our sergeant, he said, "A fine bunch of men you've got there, Sergeant" and to a lad in Number 1 Platoon, he commented, "I bet you don't stand so stiffly in the presence of your girlfriend ". He was just as informal after the marchpast, chatting away to the parents, including my Mum and Dad.

The weather remained fine in Devizes after the 7-Week Inspection and until after the day of our Passing Out Parade, but the same could certainly not be said for the Lynton and Lynmouth area of North Devon, when a devastating flash flood struck the area on the night of 15th August. There was a massive rainstorm that night, when 9-inches of rain fell. A 12-foot wall of water raced down from the Exmoor Hills, which caused the East and West Lyn Rivers to burst their banks. 90-Million tons of water carried boulders and trees through the village, destroying many homes and killing 36 people.

Amazingly enough, I did not hear about this terrible disaster until some days later, as I did not see a newspaper all the time I was in the Training Centre and the barrack rooms of the trainees did not possess a radio.

I left the Training Centre two days after the Passing Out Parade, but remained at the Camp for the next five weeks, as I had put down my name to go on a Burroughs Accounting Machine Course, which was to last five weeks. I had used a Burroughs in the Bank and I think that was why my application was successful. After I had passed my Course, I was posted to Piddlehinton Camp near Dorchester. This Pay Office handled the accounts of all RASC personnel (apart from the Commisioned Officers) and I believe accounts of officers were handled at the Manchester Pay Office.

I saw a little more of my home when I was at Piddlehinton, as I used to go home on the monthly 48-hour leave and at the beginning of November was granted a week's privilege leave.

But, I was certainly glad that I was breathing pure Piddlehinton air and not the Sydenham air from Friday 5th December to Tuesday 9th, for on 5th December, a terrible thick pea-soup fog descended on London. This noxious fog killed around 4,000 people, mainly the elderly. I recently read an article about the Great London Smog, the writer's reasoning being that the very still air and the burning of tarred wooden blocks had caused such a pea-souper The last tram had run in London the previous July and then all the tram tracks were torn up. These had been held in place by these wooden blocks, which had been discarded and left on the side of the road, thus providing free fuel for a grateful public.

There was soon to be another flood disaster at the start of the following year.

St. Mary's Church, Piddlehinton, February 1954.

Chapter Five

FLOODS, FREEZE UP AND FORKED LIGHTNING

On the night of 31st January 1953, the east coast of England suffered one of the worst floods in living memory. Throughout the evening, fresh winds and high tides pushed the sea to dangerous levels, flood defences were breached by huge waves and coastal towns in Kent, Essex, Suffolk, Norfolk and Lincolnshire were devastated by sea water. Over 300 people lost their lives and over 24,000 houses were flooded.

Around 40,000 people were evacuated from their homes, many of whom had to spend the freezing cold night sitting on their rooftops awaiting rescue by the fire brigade, the police, the Army and the RNLI. My wife had an aunt, uncle and cousin who lived at Jaywick, near Clacton-on-Sea, Essex and they had to spend the night sitting on the roof of their bungalow before they were rescued

I remember the spring and summer of 1953 as being one of the wettest, coldest and most miserable ones that I can remember. I was, of course, still doing my National Service and at that time stationed at Piddlehinton Camp, near Dorchester, Dorset. We literally had a heatwave lasting just one day; I think it was in July! The temperature must have been in the upper eighties, although it was not too bad during the day, as working in the office; the stone floors tended to keep the building cool. But, the temperature had scarcely dropped by the evening and Captain Sleeman, our Company Commander, had ordered us all to 'barrack bash', which meant cleaning our barrack rooms thoroughly, inside and out.

Our Corporal had detailed me to clean the outside windows, so out I went with a sponge, a cloth and one of our fire buckets in the blazing heat and started to clean the windows. A few moments later, Captain Sleeman appeared, checking on how I was getting on. "It's damned hot, King", he said, "I expect you would like to cool your feet, in that bucket".

"Yes, Sir", I said and I certainly would have, as one's feet became very hot and sweaty in heavy Army boots during a heatwave. The next day, however, the weather was back to normal.

I remember one pleasant weekend at the end of August. Although there was no heatwave then, the weather was quite hot and sunny and my best friend Malcolm and I decided to spend the weekend at Weymouth. We had to work on the Saturday morning; so we caught a train from Dorchester South station at around two o'clock in the afternoon. Weymouth was only eight miles from Dorchester, so we soon arrived there, booking into a bed and breakfast for one night at the Salvation Army Hostel in the town. We were allowed to leave our belongings, then we made a beeline for the beach. I mention that B&B cost us just 2/6d each!

We spent most of the weekend swimming and sunbathing. It was pleasantly warm, without being too hot. Weymouth possesses the best beach that I know, with lovely sands and the water is the clearest that I have seen. Otherwise, I recall the weather being dismal that year and even Coronation Day was not favoured with good weather.

It was Tuesday 2nd June, when Queen Elizabeth was crowned in Westminster Abbey. The CO had given everybody the day off, except those who were on duty at the Camp.

I would have liked to have gone to London to watch the processions and taken part in the festivities, but the CO would not allow anybody to travel to London, his reasoning being that some chaps might get carried away with the festivities and miss the last train back to Dorchester, thus being AWOL (Absent Without Leave).

I decided, therefore, to spend the day in Bournemouth, as Captain Rapson, my boss in the office, who lived in Bournemouth, was organising a double-decker bus to take some of the men to the town. There was a big demand for tickets and Malcolm I and four other friends, quickly decided that we would like to go there.

The bus left camp at 10.00 hours and arrived at Bournemouth Square about an hour later and after alighting from the bus, we made straight for the beach. It was a dull and rather cold day and we sat in a shelter on the prom near Bournemouth Pier.

To our astonishment, one lad began stripping off to his bathing trunks. He then raced onto the beach then straight into the sea, although he soon came out again - with his teeth chattering! That spring and summer, we had scarcely any hot weather to warm the sea up.

When the lad had dressed himself, we all walked along the zigzag path along the East Cliff to Boscombe. We arrived there about midday, when it started to rain heavily and we decided that it was a good idea to have some lunch, so we went into a nearby cafe. When we came out it was still raining, even more heavily and the sky was a steely grey, all around, so it did not look like stopping.

Anyway, we then decided that there was nothing for it, but to spend the afternoon in the Cinema. I cannot now remember the name of the cinema, but it was situated in the corner of a shopping arcade in Boscombe. I think that the arcade is still there, but the cinema has long gone. I cannot now recall the film we saw either.

When we came out of the cinema, it had stopped raining and we returned to the same cafe for some tea. From what I remember, the evening was the most pleasant part of the day, so we sat for quite time in Boscombe Gardens, until, in fact, the illuminations came on. I thought the lights were quite impressive, as located in the trees and bushes, were coloured bulbs in the shape of various animals

It was then time to walk back to Bournemouth to catch our bus, which was scheduled to leave at 11 p.m. from the Square. Once we arrived there, there was just time for a quick pint in the Windsor Tavern, before walking the short distance to the Square. Although the bus had hard wooden sheets, I slept like a log on the journey back to the Camp.

Back in London, the Coronation ceremony was impressive and memorable and afterwards, a procession of carriages accompanied by military and naval contingents passed through the streets of London. In these carriages rode foreign Heads of State and other VIPs. However, by this time, it was raining hard which was a pity, as the crowds would have been able to see an even more colourful procession if the weather had been fine and the carriages had been open to the skies.

But, there was one exception - Queen Salote of Tonga insisted on leaving her carriage open. Queen Salote was the only reigning queen in the Commonwealth, apart from our own dear Queen. Queen Salote was wearing a magnificent pink robe and a head-dress of feathers and was, indeed, a colourful sight as she rode through the streets of London, her face wreathed in smiles. The crowd took her to their hearts and cheered her enthusiastically and I not think that anybody who is old enough to remember the Coronation will forget the Queen of Tonga. Indeed, after the Coronation, someone wrote a song about her.

I recall that the winter of 1953-54 was generally mild until the last week in January. At the beginning of that week, there was a General Inspection at the Camp, when all Companies had to parade on the Square at 09.00 hours to await the arrival of the great man . It was very cold and we had been standing to attention for some time, awaiting the General's arrival, when suddenly I felt faint and blacked out. I came to quite quickly, to find the soldier next to me holding me up. I silently thanked him as I did not want to draw attention to myself.

I had been very fortunate, insofar as all the officers and NCOs were in front of the men and facing the front, waiting for the General to arrive, so that none of my superiors had noticed that I had temporarily passed out. I had had breakfast that morning, so I doubt that I would have been put on a charge for fainting on parade (but, somone that had gone without his breakfast, would have been). Shortly afterwards, the General arrived and fortunately, he did not take long to inspect us and then the march past soon warmed me up. As far as I can recall, we passed our Inspection with the General being satisfied with our turnout, barrack rooms and kit layouts.

On the day after the Inspection, it started to snow heavily and continued right up to the Friday, when most chaps been given a 48-hour leave pass. At 11.00 hours that afternoon, I walked down to the square and saw the three Bere Regis coaches that were going to London. I approached the driver of one of them, who did not seem very optimistic. "I don't know whether I will be able to get you lads to London", he said, "I can't take our usual route, as Salisbury has been cut off because of snow drifts, so I will have to try to get to London via the New Forest and Winchester".

So, we set off and eventually, we reached the New Forest. I recall the conditions being very dangerous there, with vehicles using snow-chains. I remember when travelling across a particularly bleak and treeless part of the forest, a friend of mine - by the name of Ted White - looking out of the coach window and exclaiming, "Russia!". I looked out at the snowy wilderness and it certainly looked like photographs of Russia that I had seen. Luckily, we had a good driver and he got us to London in one piece and surprisingly not too late in view of the conditions.

I remember Gran remarking what a bitterly cold wind there was that weekend and as normally Gran was a hardy person, it must have been cold. I certainly felt cold when I went to Penge shopping on the Saturday afternoon and I was glad to get home out of the bitterly cold wind. For the first time since December 1952, I wore my warm uniform to go home, as you were allowed to wear one's civvies, after completing six months service.

I thought that we might have been snowed in for a few days, with a bit of luck and thus have a few more days at home, but I think that it was too cold to snow, so I caught a train to Waterloo East on the Sunday night and walked the short distance to an old bomb-site, opposite the Old Vic, where our coach was waiting to take us back to camp.

The snow, however, came cascading down and the following day, a new duty was introduced to us: 'brazier duty'. The CO had been worried about the washrooms and latrines freezing up in the exceptionally cold weather, so some lads were detailed to place a coke brazier in each washroom and lavatory. These were to be kept going at night by a chap who had to walk round who at night stoking up these braziers. Now Piddlehinton Camp was a bleak and open camp with washrooms and latrines dotted all over it. So, it was a particularly disagreeable duty trudging round the camp in the bitter night-time temperatures keeping these braziers alight. I noticed that my name was on this rota for one night in the middle of the following week, so I fervently hoped there would be a thaw by then! It was so cold that week, my shaving brush, which I kept on the top of my locker, froze in the overnight temperatures and the water in the fire buckets in the barrack room, froze over at night also.

But, the coldest day of this cold snap was on the Thursday of that week. I walked out of my barrack room at 06.45 hours that morning, wearing my battle-dress and my warm greatcoat to go to breakfast, but walking up to the cookhouse, I felt that 'I was wearing nothing, the wind was so bitter.

On Thursday evenings I used to go to Evening Classes at the Corn Exchange in Dorchester, with a friend by the name of Robert Allen. We caught a camp bus at around 6.30 p.m., just outside the Guardroom. Somehow our driver managed to get us to Dorchester, in spite of the snow and ice and we then got off the bus and walked across the road to

The Corn Exchange. Once we were seated in our classroom, our tutor said, "Thank you all for making the effort to get here. The temperature in Dorchester today has been 1deg Fahrenheit" (i.e. 31 degrees of frost!).

This was about the third or fourth time that we had attended these classes. On the first night, Robert had become friendly with a girl, who used to travel up from Weymouth. With the classes finishing at 8 o'clock and the camp bus not leaving Dorchester until 10, Robert said that he would walk the girl back to Dorchester South station and see her on to the train for Weymouth. I would walk to the station with them, but, not wishing to play gooseberry, I left Robert to make his fond farewells on the Down platform, while I sat in the waiting room reading. When Robert returned, there was just enough time for us to buy a hot pork-pie each at the fish and chip shop, before walking the short distance to the Bere Regis bus terminus.

But on this particular Thursday, Robert's girlfriend had not risked travelling up from Weymouth in such bad conditions, so we had nothing to do after 8 o'clock. We did not want to wait in the bitter cold for two hours until our bus was due. In addition, Thursday was early-closing day in the town and in those days, early closing meant just that. You couldn't even get a cup of tea in the town on a Thursday afternoon or evening. So, Robert and I decided to walk the 5 miles or so, through the snowy wilderness back to camp. Somehow, we managed to get back in one piece and we then went to the NAAFI and thawed ourselves out with hot cups of tea.

The cold snap lasted until the middle of the following week, the miraculous thaw that I had been hoping for arriving on the day before my night-time brazier duty. So I, therefore, got out of doing this unpleasant duty. Because there had been so much snow, there was plenty of slush on the Camp for about a week or so.

The rest of February and March was generally quite cold, but April was a lovely warm month. I spent most of Easter at Malcolm's house, his parents living at Walsall, his parents and his sister, Doreen making me very welcome. On Good Friday, Malcolm and I visited a well-known local beauty spot, Cannock Chase. It was a nice afternoon, but the wind was a bit keen. I always found the Midlands generally colder than London and indeed, Dorchester.

On the Saturday, Malcolm's father took us to The Hawthorns to see West Bromwich Albion play Manchester City, with WBA winning the match by one goal to nil. The following week, WBA were to win the FA Cup at Wembley, beating Preston North End by two goals to one. Easter Sunday was my birthday and I received some nice cards and presents from Malcolm and his family.

Unfortunately, I had to return to Piddlehinton Camp that night, as I was on Guard Duty the next day. It was a lovely day and I found a Bank Holiday Guard Duty far more relaxing than a normal one. Robert Allen was also on duty and the Guard Commander allowed him to bring his gramophone and his excellent collection of jazz records into the Guardroom. Somehow, they wired up the system to the Guardroom loudspeakers and jazz blared out over part of the Camp all day. The Guard commander told Robert to unplug the system round about 18.00 hours as some officers would soon start returning to the camp.

Of course, I had to do a stint of two hours sentry duty every six hours, but otherwise things were very relaxed and apart from the person on sentry duty and the two men patrolling the camp on picket, everyone else was allowed to lay out on the lawn at the back of the guardroom that lovely afternoon. As mentioned, Robert Allen was in the Guard contingent and there was another chap there by the name of Ray Stewart.

He was tall, dark and good-looking and I thought he bore a great resemblance to Cary Grant. He was also very smart, having been an ex-Champion recruit at the Training Centre. I used to envy him his looks (his parting was always immaculate like Cary Grant) and taking his beret on and off did not seem to make his hair tousled like the rest of us. He also possessed the same easy charm of Grant. By rights, having been a Champion Recruit, he should have attained the rank of Training Centre Sergeant, but apparently had been made a Lance-Corporal in the Centre, but was busted to Private for some reason and sent to Piddlehinton Camp. He was very demob happy, as he had just 10 days to do.

May was a very pleasant month, but the weather still had one dirty trick up its sleeve. One afternoon, I had just returned to the office after lunch, when the sky started to darken. Suddenly, it started to rain torrentially and this was accompanied' by forked lightning and heavy thunder. With that, Captain Rapson told us all to unplug our machines.

A chap by the name of Bill stretched over a desk to unplug his machine, when, suddenly, there was a flash and a bang and Bill collapsed stunned on his desk. Fortunately, he came to after a few moments. Also, fortunately, the storm soon abated and with that the Captain detailed somebody to take Bill to the MI room. He was checked over by the MO who, thankfully, pronounced him A1.

I was very demob happy that month and I spent most of the lovely light evenings walking with some of my mates down to The New Inn at Piddlehinton and then walking back, feeling merry in the honeysuckle-scented night air back to camp. I had two demob parties; one on 12th

June at The George, Dorchester for the chaps in my barrack room and another one on 14th June for the chaps from my Intake. I was duly demobbed on Thursday 17th June.

I was awarded $3^{1/2}$ weeks paid demob leave, but only took $2^{1/2}$ weeks break. I spent some time at home and then spent a week's holiday at Shanklin on the Isle of Wight with my parents, before returning to work in the bank on 5th July. I had been transferred from the Edgware Road branch of the bank to the main London Office in Lombard Street, EC3.

After demob. I was placed on the Army Emergency Reserve for $3^{1/2}$ years and I would have to attend one AER camp of a fortnight's duration per year. The weather remained mild throughout the remainder of 1954 and the beginning of 1955, until just before my first AER Camp on 19th February and then we had a cold snap of over a fortnight equal in severity to the one we had the previous year.

Picture of the author taken at snow covered barracks
at Canterbury, February 1955.

Chapter Six

WOMENS' QUARTERS, WARM BEER AND WRETCHED JELLYFISH

At the beginning of February 1955, I received a letter in the post telling me 'to report on 19th February to Chaucer Barracks Canterbury for a fortnight AER Camp'. Also enclosed, was a rail warrant reserving me a seat on the 1.15 p.m. train from Charing Cross to Canterbury West on that date.

It had been snowing heavily two or three days before I was due to report for my AER Camp and in addition, I had the worst cold that I can remember. I was thinking of going to my GP and asking him for a certificate excusing me from this camp, but I was getting worked up about putting on a uniform again and submitting again to Army discipline and did not want to experience that feeling again later in the year.

So, on 19th February there was really nothing for it, but to make my way to Charing Cross station with my kitbag on my shoulder to catch the 1.15p.m. train. We were allowed to report to the camp in civvies provided, of course, that we put on our uniform for our first parade and wore it thereafter for all military activities. I felt wretched on the journey down, however, and was thinking of reporting sick when I arrived at the camp. But, then, an amazing thing made me change my mind. I started to read a magazine which I had bought at W. H. Smith's at Charing Cross station and I came across a report of an interview given by the famous actor Douglas Fairbanks Jnr. to a reporter from the magazine. Apparently he was ill with the 'flu but insisted on carrying on with the interview. Now, Fairbanks was one of my favourite actors and I thought that if he could carry on with the 'flu, I could carry on with a heavy cold.

In due course, the train arrived at Canterbury West station and I immediately noticed that the snow was deeper than the snow in London. So, I gingerly made my way across the icy station concourse with my kitbag on my shoulder and climbed aboard a waiting Army lorry, which was to take us to Chaucer Barracks. It was a fairly short drive to the Barracks and when we arrived there, we were told to fall in threes. There were two platoons of Reservists and the Sergeant instructed each man which platoon he was in and which barrack room.

I then made my way to my barrack room and the Corporal-in-charge told us all to stand by our beds. He told us to make our beds and put our kit in our lockers. He then detailed two men to take a coal-scuttle to the coal yard and fill it with wood and coal. The barrack room was freezing cold, but when they came back, they had a job to get the fire going, as the wood had been lying in deep snow. Eventually, they succeeded in lighting the fire, but the small coal fire at one end of the room made little difference, unless you were sitting on top of it.

The Corporal then said, "You can go to tea now lads and after that, the evening is yours. You can remain in your civvies, but you will parade at 08.00hrs. *sharp* in your uniform outside the barrack room". I was glad just to get a mug of tea in the cook-house to warm me up.

Two of my best friends from the Training Centre and Piddlehinton Camp - Tiny Taylor and Pete Dowling - were in my barrack room. And we all agreed we would like to walk to Canterbury and find a pub with a roaring fire, where we could warm ourselves up. Another two chaps came with us and we all walked down to the city through the snow. We came across an attractive-looking pub near a bridge over the River Stour in the City Centre, which was called The Oporto. Going inside, we were fascinated to see that all the tables and chairs were made out of varnished and polished beer barrels. The tables were complete barrels and the chairs were barrels, which had been sculpted out. As its name suggests, the pub specialised in port, but sold most other drinks also. I was fond of port in those days and two or three glasses of the stuff seated in front of a roaring fire, warmed me up and made my cold feel much better. The landlord was a friendly chap; he was smart, brisk and business-like and put me very much in mind of my Uncle Jim.

But soon, I began to feel ill again, so I told Tiny, Pete and the others that I was going back to camp to get my head down. I walked out of the pub and trudged about a mile and a half through the snow and ice until I reached Military Road. Now there were several barracks in that area, including ours and they all looked the same in the deep snow. I suddenly spied a sentry inside his box in front of a gate and I thought to myself 'This must be our barracks'. With that, I approached the sentry box, the sentry immediately sprang out and poked a sten-gun into my chest. He (she) shouted, "Halt! Who goes there?".

"Private King. I am an Army Emergency Reservist, attached to the Royal Army Pay Corps barracks."

"This is the Womens' Royal Army Corps barracks", she said severely, "Your barracks are over there", she said pointing towards them. I thanked her and walked over to our barracks. I felt certain that she thought that I was trying to break into the Womens' Quarters, but I felt far too rough to chase women that night and just wanted to get my head down. When I reached my barrack-room, I lost no time in getting into bed and after a good night's sleep felt a little better in the morning.

As instructed, we lined-up in three ranks outside our barrack-room at 08.00hrs. Suddenly, our Sergeant called us to attention. A young Second Lieutenant appeared, accompanied by a burly Sergeant Major. The Sergeant yelled out the command, "Open Order March" and the Officer and the Sergeant Major started to inspect us. We were a scruffy bunch of Reservists, who were only at Chaucer Barracks for a fortnight and didn't really care. Our turnout did not impress the Officer and Warrant Officer.

I think that the young officer had been in my intake and he said to me, "You should introduce your boots to some blacking". Well, although I might have been a scruffy Reservist, I did not like my appearance criticised.

As it was a Sunday, we were let off work for the rest of the day after the Officer's inspection - and a pep talk from the Sergeant Major - in which he outlined our programme for the fortnight. So, as I had all this free time to spare, I went to the NAAFI and bought some dusters, boot polish, Brasso and Blanco and thoroughly cleaned my kit. I felt smarter and received no more adverse criticism on the morning inspection.

The Sergeant Major did not seem to like National Servicemen in general and scruffy Reservists in particular. He called some of the chaps 'wimps', as they had reported to the MO with chapped hands. I was not one of them, but it was bitterly cold and we were not allowed to wear gloves for rifle drill.

I could write another couple of pages about this fortnight camp, but as this book is mainly about the weather, I will just stick to stories about it.

The weather was bitter all over Britain during this fortnight. Although I thought that it was cold enough in Canterbury, one night when I was watching the weather report on television at The Oporto, the temperature in the Highlands of Scotland was -13degF. We liked The Oporto so much that we did not drink anywhere else during the whole fortnight.

We seemed to have a set routine at the camp during the day. In the mornings, we had military activities, such as drill and weapon training and in the afternoon helped out in the Pay Office. Being a qualified Burroughs Machinist, I was detailed to work in the Machine Section and as this Pay Office handled the accounts of the RAPC, I found myself machining the statements of some of my old mates. So, that was where I had been getting my statement from when I was at Piddlehinton camp!

On the middle Sunday, we had to visit the Open Range at Teynham near Faversham, Kent. The snow had stopped falling by then, but it was still bitterly cold. The range was situated on bleak open ground bordering the River Swale and as I was in the last detail to fire my sten gun, by that time, my hands were so numb with cold that I missed the target altogether.

We each had to do a Guard Duty during that fortnight. I had to do mine in the middle of the second week and I had to do two shifts of two hours each in the Sentry Box during the freezing cold night. All in all, I was not sorry to get home from that camp. I did not know this at the time, but Saturday March 5th 1955 was the last time I would wear a uniform and the last time that I would see Tiny Taylor and Pete Dowling, as shortly after that camp, they disbanded the AER Scheme. I kept in touch with both of them for about two years, but sadly we lost contact. I received a 21st Birthday card from Pete.

The freezing cold weather in February and March was forgotten when a most glorious summer followed. In September, the previous year, I had started to attend dancing classes at the Jimmy Small School of Dancing in Sydenham, the main purpose of which was to meet girls. I had met a girl there by the name of Ann and at the end of April, I asked her out and much to my surprise, she accepted my invitation. We went to the Capitol Cinema in Forest Hill on the following Saturday and as we both liked the cinema, we used to go to the Capitol every Saturday night during that glorious summer. We used to walk back to Ann's house in the balmy night air and I cannot remember any rain during the time we went out.

I used to see her on Monday nights at Jimmy Small's, but apart from that, we used to only go out on Saturdays. She was only 17 and studying for her Advanced Level exams, so her parents were quite strict with her. They did, however, let me take her out on Whit Monday and we went to see Motor Racing at the Crystal Palace and when her exams were finished, her parents let me see a little more of her.

One Sunday in July, we went on a coach trip to Littlehampton and it was a glorious day. However, I thought that our coach looked a little decrepit and when the coach reached Bury hill, near Arundel, it stopped halfway up the hill and would not go any further. So, the driver asked us all to get out and walk to the top of the hill in the blazing heat. The coach then proceeded up the hill empty, apart from the. driver. We all then boarded the coach again and it proceeded on its journey to Littlehampton without any further incident. The main beach was very crowded, so we spent that glorious day on the quieter West Beach on the other side of the River Arun.

I had also joined the previous September, a tennis club in Kent House Lane, Beckenham, which was attached to the Sydenham and Parkside cricket clubs. I had not played tennis much after the end of October, as I did not like playing in very cold weather and then changing in freezing cold dressing rooms, but I really lapped up my tennis in the glorious summer weather of that year.

But, there was one thing that spoilt it for me after my games of tennis and that was warm beer. The beer seemed to be warm all the time in that boiling hot summer, the reason being, of course, that there were no refrigerated shelves to keep the bottles of beer on or cool glass cabinets to keep them in. Also, we had one of those old fashioned cricket pavilions which was raised a little way off the ground with bricks and I remember as a small boy, crawling underneath the pavilion.

My mother had belonged to that tennis club until 1941, when incendiary bombs had destroyed all the grass courts. These had been replaced with hard courts in 1954. My mother played at that time at the Sydenham Gas Works club, as my father worked for the gas company. Therefore, there would have been no cool cellar under the bar. Strangely enough, I did not experience warm beer during the cooler summers of

1956/7/8 and in 1959, when we had our next blazing hot summer. For reasons that I cannot now recall, I hardly played any tennis.

Things were going well with Ann and I and in July, Ann's parents asked me if I would like to spend a weekend with them at their holiday bungalow at Bexhill-on-Sea on August. 19th-20th. I thanked them and said "Yes", but it was slightly awkward, as I had promised to go on a fortnight's Summer Camp with the Troop at Small Dole, a hamlet situated near Shoreham-on-Sea, Sussex. But, I needn't have worried. Ron D., our skipper, gave me his blessing to leave early and suggested that I caught a bus from outside of the campsite to Brighton and then catch a train to Bexhill. We had an excellent Summer Camp in glorious weather and we frequently went swimming at Shoreham-by-Sea and had two lovely days out in Brighton.

But the weather had forgotten the script on the 19th; the day that the Troop had to strike camp and the day that I had to get to Bexhill, it was pouring with rain when we got up that morning and continued all day. I managed to get to Bexhill on time, however, and Ann met me at the station. We then had a lovely lunch, as I recall, but the rain was so torrential in the afternoon, that we abandoned all thoughts of going out and stayed in and played cards all afternoon with Ann's father and brother. The rain had scarcely eased off after tea, but we felt fed up with having to stay indoors, so we went to the Curzon Cinema in the town to see Fred Astaire and Lesley Caron in 'Daddy Long-Legs'.

I awoke next morning to see that normal weather service had resumed - it was a lovely day. Ann was a prodigious walker and once we walked £or about seven miles around Sydenham, Crystal Palace and Beckenham. So, I felt somewhat apprehensive when she announced that we were going on one of her 'walks'. She said that we were going to walk along the beach from Bexhill to Hastings and back (a distance of around ten miles). When we arrived at Hastings, Ann looked at her watch and said we had better catch a bus back, otherwise we would not be back in time for lunch. I was so sorry!

In the afternoon, we all decided to go swimming. It was a lovely hot afternoon and we raced into the sea. But, we did not stay in the water long, as it was teeming with jellyfish. Apparently, the hot summer had attracted them to the waters off the South coast and I think that most of them must have been in the waters off Bexhill!

After tea, it was time for me to return home. Ann saw me off at the station and we seemed to have spent an enjoyable weekend together, so it came as a big surprise to me, when I rang her once she had returned from her holiday and found that she did not seem to want to go out with me any more. But, I understood when she said that she was too young to want to get serious with anybody at the moment. She did, however, go out with me one more time and that was to the wedding of Tim, the former Cubmaster and Dorothy, who was an Assistant Cub leader in the St. Michael's Cub Pack. I appreciated this, as I would have lost face turning up at the wedding without her. Immediately after that, we broke up without acrimony. I had liked and respected her.

Brenda and I setting off for an outing on my Lambretta, Summer 1957.

Chapter Seven

ON A PERSONAL
(NOT A WEATHER) FRONT

In order to give my book some continuity, I hope that the reader will forgive me if I give some brief details of some personal events in my life, as there seemed to be little extraordinary weather between the hot summer of 1955 and the fine, dry and at times, hot summer of 1957. I feel that to jump from one extraordinary spell of weather to another without writing anything else in between, would make my story somewhat disjointed.

I felt rather depressed after breaking up with Ann and tried to occupy my spare time with plenty of social activities. I ceased to go to Jimmy Small's, however, as I would have found it rather embarrassing seeing her there.

I had my Scouting activities, of course and I continued to play tennis regularly until the end of October. I did not play much after that until the following April, as I did not really enjoy playing in the cold weather and then changing in the freezing dressing-room.

I started to go to more social functions, such as the Sydenham and Parkside Cricket Club's End of Season Dance. My attending this dance came about in rather a strange way. It was Saturday, October 1st and the Vicar was holding a 'mile of pennies' event at the site of the old church. The church had been destroyed by German bombs on 9th October 1940 and since that time, services had been held at the Church Hall in Bell Green, Sydenham. The rebuilding of a new church was to commence at any time and the Vicar needed funds for the refurbishment of the new church. It was a beautiful early October day and a lot of people came to this event, the object of which was to try to make a circle of pennies around Champion Crescent which surrounded the site of the old church. The Scouters played an active part in this event, supervising the laying down of the pennies (and making sure that none were pinched!).

Now, Mum knew that I had been feeling depressed after the break-up with Ann and said to me, "The Sydenham and Parkside Cricket Clubs have an End of Season Dance tonight. Dad and I are going. Why don't you ask your fellow Scouters if they are free tonight and whether they would like to come?".

"I don't suppose any of them will be able to at such short notice", I remember replying. Anyway, I asked my fellow Scouters and their wives and girlfriends, who were also present at the event, if they would like to come and amazingly they all said "Yes".

So, a party of nine of us went in the end and we all had a very enjoyable time. In fact, I enjoyed myself so much that I attended every single dance that they held during the rest of the 1950s, apart from the New Year's Eve dance in 1956, when I had to work very late at the Bank on 'balance' work. The clubs ran three dances a year: The End of Season dance, New Year's Eve and the Beginning of the Season Dance.

I also started to go to jazz concerts at the Gaumont Cinema, Lewisham, with the same group of people who had attended the Cricket Club Dance. We used to attend Evensong at St. Michael's in Bell Green. This finished around 7.30 p.m. and we then used to cross the road and catch a number 108 bus to Lewisham. The jazz concerts used to start at 8 o'clock and I think that we went about five times. We listened to the bands of Ted Heath, Ray Anthony and Ken Mackintosh, but I cannot now remember the names of the other two bands. I went to a very good Christmas Dance at the King Alfred, Bellingham with Ron D and his wife, Margaret and

Ron S and his girlfriend Pat.

But, by 1956, I was tiring of the social life without a girlfriend. And I thought that the answer might be to acquire some transport. So, in June I bought a second-hand motor-scooter - a Lambretta.

The following month Mum, Dad, Geoff and I moved from the house which we shared with Miss Hare and moved in with Gran, who lived nearby, who I think was lonely. I think that July 1956 was the first time she had lived alone that century. Gran and Grandad had married at the end of the previous one and she had lived with him until March 1945, when he was killed by a V2 rocket while working in Smithfield market. Then Auntie Jean and Uncle Bill lived with her until the beginning of 1956, when they moved to a house close by to Uncle Bill's parents. Just after that, my Auntie Ciss and Uncle Jim came to live there for a few months, while they were waiting for a new bungalow to be built in Barnehurst, Kent. So, at the beginning of July, Gran was alone and she asked Mum and Dad if they would like to move in with her and they both agreed to. We all got on very well with Gran and I cannot remember her ever saying a cross word to me.

Our Summer Camp was spent in a field belonging to a farmer in Sedlescombe, a village situated near Hastings. I went to camp on my scooter and was able to get about on it. The weather was mainly miserable that week, as was most of the summer, as I recall. I missed my old girlfriend and decided to send her a postcard while I was away at Summer Camp. Just after the breakup, I saw her out with a new boyfriend, but I had heard that she was no longer seeing him and I wondered what were the chances of getting back with her?

On 15th November, I passed my Scooter Test and then plucked up the courage to ask her out. She accepted and we made a date for the Saturday week 24th November, which was her birthday. I cannot now remember what I bought her, but we went to the State Cinema in Sydenham (which was just a few doors away from where she lived) to see Yul Brynner and Deborah Kerr in 'The King and I'. By the oddest of coincidences, the movie was 'Raising a Riot' starring Kenneth More, which happened to be the second feature the very first time we went out in April 1955.

I was invited to Ann's aunt and uncle for tea on Christmas Day and we had a very enjoyable time. At one stage, Ann's father said to me, "Look out of the window, Michael. It's snowing". There were a few flakes coming down and soon it stopped snowing altogether and I remember wondering whether one qualified for a payout if one had placed a bet on it snowing on Christmas Day, or whether the snowfall would have had to be more substantial as it was on Christmas Day 1970.

Ann and I seemed to be getting on well again. We went to the cinema quite often, but on some Saturday nights in the first three months of 1957, we went to Saturday dances at the Royston Ballroom in Beckenham, which was owned by Frank and Peggy Spencer of 'Come Dancing' fame.

But sadly, our friendship was not to last. I was an Assistant Scoutmaster in the Troop and was in charge of the Senior Scouts. There was quite a heavy Scouting programme in March and April and on Saturday 2nd March, I had to take my lads to a meeting of Senior Scouts from Troops in the County of London. There were many Scouting 'Brass-hats' there, including the County Commissioner. I was unable to go out with Ann that day, as this event took up the afternoon and evening.

On Sunday 31st March, I rode down on my scooter with John on the back to Kingsdown, a coastal village between Deal and Dover. As Ron H and Ron S also owned Lambrettas, they came as well. Ron D had instructed us to have a look at the Scout Association camp at Kingsdown and if we liked the site, to book a camping site for the forthcoming Summer Camp in August. We liked the site, so we duly made the booking with the Bailiff. I was out all day and just about made it to Evensong, where I arrived in a somewhat scruffy state, after having got home late due to mechanical trouble with the scooter. Naturally, when I met Ann and her parents there, they were not impressed.

The last straw however in our relationship was Easter Camp. I had arranged to take Ann out on the Good Friday, but was going to camp for the rest of Easter. After a big row about it, we broke up. It had been entirely my fault and I was ashamed at the way I had taken her for granted over Easter Camp. But, I was fairly committed to Scouting in those days and if I had tried to get back with her, I could see further problems in our relationship and I respected her far too much to put her second most of the time. Most of my fellow Scouters had wives and girlfriends who were involved in Cub, Scouting or Guide activities which made their relationships somewhat easier.

I felt very depressed that Easter and there was no way that I felt like going to Frylands Woods camp on that Good Friday. Besides, I could keep stumm for a little longer about what had happened and therefore 'save face'. I went to camp on the Saturday, but felt depressed and did not really enjoy it.

I felt that I needed a holiday. On June 8th, Mum and Dad had booked a holiday for themselves and my brother - Geoff - at a holiday camp at Brighstone on the Isle of Wight. Coincidentally, I was due for a week's leave from work that week and I asked my parents if I could come along, provided that the camp had a vacancy. I think that Mum rang the holiday camp and fortunately, they did have one.

The holiday soon arrived. Mum and Dad went down to Portsmouth by train, then over the ferry to Ryde, where the Camp coach met them. Geoff rode on the pillion of the scooter and we travelled down to Lymington, where we took a ferry to Yarmouth.

It was a typical 'Hi-de-hi' type holiday camp. We were woken up each morning with "Good morning, campers" over the Tannoy. We ended the day with "Good night, campers" in the ballroom and there was such events as 'The Knobbly-knees Contest'. But, I enjoyed my week there, thanks to Mike the Camp Organiser, a very energetic and charismatic man, who organised rambles, coach trips, tennis and putting competitions, as well as organising all the evening activities. I returned from my week's holiday feeling much better.

I had been friendly for some time with a girl by the name of Brenda, who worked on the same floor as me in the bank, but in a different department. I had, in fact, known her since July 1954, when I returned to the Bank to work in the main London Office.

So, on Sunday 30th June, I travelled down on my scooter to her home in Meopham, Kent. Her parents made me very welcome and her mother cooked an excellent Sunday dinner. It was exceptionally hot that day, with temperatures just over 90degF and I was glad to feel a cool breeze on my face as I sped along on my scooter. After Sunday dinner, we went on a two-mile walk in the lovely countryside of Meopham. We walked over the fields to Meopham Green and then back again. But, the heat made walking very tiring and we were glad to get back into the relative coolness of the bungalow, where Brenda and her family lived. At around 9 p.m. I rode back to Sydenham in the cool night air, having had a most enjoyable day.

The temperature remained in the upper eighties during the following week. On the Saturday, Miss Hare was giving a garden party in order to raise funds for the refurbishment of the new church. Rebuilding was well under way by that time and the consecration of the new church was expected to take place the following summer. The Troop had an active role in the Garden Party and some of the Scouters and Scouts ran sideshows. I was given the job of taking the admission money at the gate with a chap by the name of David. He had no involvement with the Troop, but was a regular churchgoer. I knew him quite well, as we often used to travel on the same tram to school. He used to get off at the stop nearest to his school, Dulwich College and I used to get off a few stops later and walk up Townley Road to Alleyns School.

Before I proceed any further, I will give some background about Miss Hare, who had been our landlady between 1936, when my parents rented the ground floor at her house, until July 1956, when we moved in with Gran. Miss Hare had also been a good friend and I have written quite a lot about her in my two previous books.

The temperature was in the upper eighties that day and it was very hot standing in one place, taking the admission money. Still, things went smoothly except for one embarrassing moment. As I was busy taking the admission money, I suddenly looked up and spied in the queue, Ann and her new boyfriend. As mentioned earlier, the break-up was rather acrimonious and I did not know whether or not she would speak to me. As she approached, I looked up and smiled and thankfully she reciprocated. She then introduced her boyfriend to me and I shook his hand and wished them all the best for the future.

Eventually, the queue began to dwindle and Ron D suggested that we go somewhere to count the money. I knew the ideal place - Miss Hare's front room! It had always been a lovely cool room in the hottest weather. I knew this well, of course, because, less than a year earlier, we had lived in this room!

I would have liked Brenda to have come to the Garden Party, but she had a previous engagement as she had been invited to the wedding of one of her friends from work.

I enjoyed my Summer Camp at Kingsdown, the weather being hot and sunny, without it being unbearably hot. The beach was literally a stone's throw from the camp and we went swimming every day.

Brenda also went on holiday in August,, going to Nice for a fortnight with a friend from work and visiting many interesting places, including the Casino at Monte Carlo. We were both pleased to be back from work, so that we could start going out again. Things were going well for us in September and October, but the end of the year was to be a sad time for me.

A bus conductor walking in front of his bus with a flare in a typical London fog.

Chapter Eight

SAD TIMES

On 1st November, Gran died suddenly. It was a cold day and she had been cleaning the outside windows, when she had a severe heart attack. Somebody phoned for an ambulance and then phoned Dad, who raced home from the nearby gasworks. He went in the ambulance with Gran to Lewisham Hospital, but she died on the journey. I was told of Gran's death when I arrived home from work. I felt devastated as I had always been very fond of Gran and I cannot remember her saying a cross word to me. She had a most lovely smile, which seemed to cheer everybody up. The whole family was saddened by her death as she had been a tower of strength to us all.

On 4th December disaster struck. There was a terrible train crash at Lewisham, when two commuter trains collided in dense fog, killing 92 people. I lost a friend by the name of Pat, who was only 19 years of age.

She was always such a cheerful girl, in fact, I never knew her to be miserable. There was a group of us who used to travel to London each morning, Pat, her friend, whose name I could not remember at the time and two chaps called John and Peter; the latter being in the Scout troop a few years previously. I used to travel back with them from London whenever I could. The rest of the group got on at Charing Cross Station and used to sit towards the rear of the train. I used to walk to London Bridge Station from the Bank in time to catch this train, but by some miracle, I missed this train on the night of the crash. I had hung about at the office talking to a chap, who was a motor cycle fanatic, about scooters, which he didn't think much of.

The train that my friends were travelling on, had stopped in the fog at a red light just beyond St. John's Station. The driver of a London-Tonbridge express, which was following, failed to stop at a red light on the approach side to the station and smashed into the back of the train which my friends were on. The second coach of the express reared up with the impact and brought down a one-section steel bridge on top of it, killing almost everybody in the second coach of the Tonbridge train and there were some very severe casualties in the rear of the Hayes train. Pat was very badly injured and so was her friend and shortly afterwards, Pat died in Lewisham Hospital. There was an article and a photograph of her on the front page of the *Daily Express,* the headline reading, 'The courage of a girl called Pat'. Although in a terrible way herself, she had tried to cheer up some of the other badly injured people. I felt privileged to have been her friend for such a short time and I still have this newspaper cutting. I did not know much about Pat's friend, or where she came from, but happily I have recently found out that she made a full recovery from her injuries (please see end of Chapter).

There were 92 deaths as a result of this train crash, but unbelievably, the death toll could have been much worse. The one-section steel bridge, to which I referred earlier, carried the Holborn-Dartford trains. As the bridge crashed down on the second coach of the Tonbridge train, the driver of a train up above, just about managed to bring his train to a halt in the fog before it would have plunged into the yawning chasm on top of the Tonbridge train. Goodness knows how many deaths this would have caused?

I arrived at London Bridge station that night, knowing that I had missed my usual train. When I arrived at the top of the stairs, I noticed that there was a stationary train on each of the Down platforms and huge crowds were milling about on the platforms. Suddenly, there came an announcement, "Please do not get on these trains. There has been a serious incident outside St. John's station. Please find alternative means of getting home". Suddenly, I spied the tall and powerful figure of Ron D on the opposite platform. He saw me and shouted, "Come over here, Michael". When I arrived there he said, "The best thing to do is to walk over to the Terminus sector of the station and catch a train to Forest Hill. Any trains which would have had to go through New Cross station will be affected, but not those stopping at or going through New Cross Gate". As the Forest Hill train stopped at New Cross Gate, we were alright. We got off at Forest Hill station and walked towards Ron's house. The fog was really dense, indeed it was so bad, that bus conductors were walking in front of their buses with flares. In due course, we reached Ron's house and I walked on towards mine. When I arrived home, Mum and Dad told me what had happened. They had heard about the train crash on the radio. Malcolm, my friend from National Service days, who lived in Walsall, had also heard about the crash and phoned me to see if I was alright.

Two days later, I read about Pat in the paper and heard that her friend had been badly injured and that John had escaped serious injury. Peter had not travelled on the train that night.

I spent Christmas day with my parents and Geoff, but I could not shake off the feeling of sadness over the accident and in losing such a good friend. Brenda spent Christmas Day at her home, as our parents always insisted that Christmas Day should be spent at home. On Boxing Day, Brenda came to my home, as we always had a big party on Boxing Day to celebrate Geoff's Birthday. As I went to meet Brenda from the train at Beckenham Hill station, I felt particularly sad when I passed the end of Pat's road, which was very near the station. When Brenda and I came out of the station, we bumped into John, who was carrying his golf clubs. When we asked him how he was, he said that he was still badly shaken, but was going to play a round of golf at nearby Beckenham Place Park to try to take his mind off the terrible sights that he had seen.

At the start of 1958 I could still not get the terrible Lewisham train Crash out of my mind but on February 6th came more bad news. Manchester United had been playing a European Cup match in Belgrade and the plane on which they were travelling home stopped at Munich Airport for refuelling. It landed in a snowstorm; conditions were really bad. The airfield was covered in snow and there was slush on the runways. The plane crashed attempting to take off. It was also thought that, there had been ice on the wings of the plane. Twenty-three people were killed including eight players, five of whom were under 25 years of age. The team were known as the Busby Babes, Matt Busby himself was injured in the crash. I think that all the players that I saw play so brilliantly at Charlton in 1948 had retired, and Busby had groomed some brilliant young replacements. There was a great affection for Manchester United, their manager and the Busby Babes and this disaster seemed to affect a lot of people personally. There was such a tragic waste of young lives.

The next day, the two Rons, John and I helped Ron D. and his wife Maggie move house. They had lived with Ron's parents since their wedding in 1953 and were now moving in to a place of their own. Usually when we all got together the mood was one of hilarity, but we all felt subdued that day because of the terrible news of the previous day.

In spite of this terrible tragedy they still reached the F.A. Cup Final that year I watched this match on television and a lump came to my throat when I watched the United players run out on to the Wembley pitch to play Bolton Wanderers. I think that everybody, apart from the Bolton supporters wanted United to win but sadly they lost the match 2-0.

The Munich air crash happened so soon after the Lewisham train crash and I hoped that the rest of 1958 would bring happier times.

I will end this sad Chapter on a happy note. Now the account of the Lewisham train crash also appears in my last book 'Recollections of the 1950s'. In it I wrote 'I did not know much about Pat's friend or where she came from and I never found out whether she had recovered from her severe injuries. This book was reviewed by an Orpington based local paper; the main subject in this review being the Lewisham Train crash. The review was brought to the attention of Pat's friend by someone who knew her. She then rang me, having found out my telephone number from my publisher. I was delighted to hear that she had survived the crash and that she had made a full recovery from her terrible injuries. I found out that her name was Joan and that she now lives at Ashford in Kent with her husband. We have promised to keep in touch.

Brenda on holiday at Torquay
during the glorious Summer of 1959.

Chapter Nine

A WHITE EASTER, A STORMY SEPTEMBER AND A GLORIOUS SUMMER

In 1958, I declined to go to Easter Camp. I had lost one girlfriend over my decision to go to camp the previous Easter and I did not want to lose another.

It turned out to be a fortunate decision, because the weather at Easter in 1958, was the worst Easter weather that I can ever remember. It started snowing, as I recall, on the Thursday. Brenda and I had planned to go to Margate on the scooter on Good Friday. It was a very cold day and I set off for Meopham on the scooter. The main roads had been cleared of snow, but the side roads were still dangerous. When I arrived at Brenda's house, we decided to go to Margate by train instead and we caught a bus to Meopham station and from there we caught a train to Chatham to Margate, hauled by a steam locomotive.

We did not really enjoy ourselves at Margate, because it was so bitterly cold. I seemed to recall going home on the Friday night and being at home the next day. I remember this, because Geoff, who had gone to camp at Frylands Woods, arrived home on his bike, almost blue with cold. There had been a very heavy snowfall, I think, in the early hours of the Saturday, a great deal of heavy snow falling on the tents, Ron D being afraid that any further falls of snow would irreparably damage them. Therefore, he ordered the boys to strike camp. Apparently, Geoff had lent his gloves to another boy, who had not given them back to him. So, my brother arrived home, with his hands absolutely frozen. Later that day, the snow turned to slush and I remember paddling in about six inches of it when Mum asked me to get something for her from the back garden. As I recall, Brenda and I saw each other on the Sunday and Monday, but the weather was so cold and miserable, that we stopped in and watched television.

At the beginning of June, we went on our first holiday together, staying at a little village in North Devon, called West Buckland, which was about eight miles from Barnstaple. We stayed with some friends of Brenda's parents - Olive and Frank - and they had a son called Roy.

The weather that week was very changeable. We travelled down on the Sunday in fine weather and the next day, travelled on the scooter to Ilfracombe. The weather was lovely there, but when we returned to West Buckland, Olive told us that it had been raining there all day (West Buckland was only about 20-miles from Ilfracombe).

The next day, we set out for Lynton and Lynmouth and while we were there it rained nearly all the time. Conversely, when we returned to West Buckland, Olive said that it had been beautiful there. I recall that the weather the rest of the week was very changeable, but at least we had a dry day to travel home the 195 miles, as travelling in the rain would not have been very agreeable. In spite of the temperamental weather, we had had an enjoyable holiday.

I was unable to get the week off that year for Summer Camp, which was held at the Scout Association camp-site at Small Dole in Sussex, as it had been three years earlier, but I was able to get down for the weekend.

The summer that year was generally a miserable one and I hoped that September would produce better weather. I had another week's holiday due and on 8th September, Geoff and I were going camping for five days on a farm at Eype, a village near Bridport, Dorset. Ron D. had kindly arranged this for us as he knew the farmer, as the pre-war troop used to camp at his farm.

We had a good journey down on the scooter in pleasant weather, except for one scary incident. A bull had escaped from a field at Bentley in Hampshire and was running amok in the road. He had already caused three cars to pile up. I quickly assessed the situation. I knew that there would be no time to do a U-turn on the scooter, so I decided to race past him. I had no idea that my old scooter had such powers of acceleration!

When we arrived at the farm at Eype, we paid the farmer in advance for four nights, as we intended staying until the Friday. He then told us in which field we should pitch our camp. We put up our small ridge-tent and unpacked our belongings. We then gathered some wood, so that we could light a fire and went to the farmhouse to collect some water in our dixies. We cooked ourselves some tea and then turned in early, as we felt tired after the long journey.

The next day was warm and sunny. We went into Bridport to get some shopping, cooked ourselves a meal and then spent the rest of the day relaxing and sunbathing. In the evening, we went to the Palace Cinema in Bridport.

We went to bed around 11-p.m. The night was clear as I recall, but unfortunately, there must have been a drastic change in the weather during the night, as we awoke to find ourselves afloat in our sleeping bags. We got up, surveyed our wet bedding and decided to strike camp. I went to see the farmer to advise him of our decision and he kindly refunded us two nights camping charge. We made ourselves a cup of tea and ate something cold for breakfast as I recall. I had bought my small ridge-tent second-hand and when I had used it before, the weather had been good. I had wondered how it would stand up to bad weather? Now, I had my answer and did not use the tent again!

We set off at around 10-a.m. and I was pleased to set that, although it was still raining, it had eased off somewhat. I was worried however, about my temperamental old scooter. In really heavy rain, the water would get into the carburettor and stop the engine.

The rain was light but persistent until we reached Leatherhead, but then it started to rain torrentially again. We rode on a further two miles, until we reached Ashtead and then the scooter spluttered to a halt. The rain had got into the carburettor once again. Fortunately, I was a member of the AA and, as luck would have it, there was a phone box a few yards away. I phoned the AA at Guildford and before too long, a patrolman arrived.

After I had explained the problem to him, he tried to start the engine, but without success,. He, therefore, wheeled the scooter up a ramp into the back of his van, told us to climb aboard and then took the scooter and us to our doorstep. I thanked him and gave him a tip for 10/-, which I doubt was enough, even in those days, in view of the trouble he had taken.

The next day (Thursday) was a nice day, but Geoff and I felt tired and decided to stay indoors. The day after that, however, was gorgeous, so we decided to go by train to Brighton, as we had both had enough of my temperamental old scooter.

We caught a train from Sydenham to Norwood Junction, then another one to East Croydon and then a third to Brighton. We arrived there around midday and when we came out of the station, we noticed how hot it was getting. We had brought our swimming costumes and towels with us, but we did not fancy swimming off stony old Brighton Beach, so we walked along the front to Black Rock swimming pool, which was situated at the eastern end of Brighton, near the Undercliff Walk (he Pool no longer exists, as part of the Brighton Marina was built over it). The pool was an ideal place to be on such a hot afternoon, but we noticed that it was becoming more and more humid. We left the baths at around 4-p.m. and walked to Brighton station.

We caught a fast train to East Croydon at around 5-p.m. By this time, the sky was becoming darker and darker and within five minutes of leaving the station, it started to thunder and lightning flashed everywhere. This was to be the start of the most spectacular storm that I have ever seen. Continual forked lightning could be seen on both sides of the carriage and it was raining torrentially. Naturally, such a severe storm slowed down the progress of the train considerably and we arrived at East Croydon station about three hours late. The rain, thunder and lightning had stopped, however, and it took us less than an hour to get home from East Croydon.

I think that it must have rained heavily again during the night, because Brenda who was coming to our house the next day rang up to say that flooding had prevented the trains running on the Meopham and Gravesend lines and that she was going by bus to Gravesend to catch a Green Line Bus to Beckenham. I picked her up on my scooter outside the Regal Cinema and while I was waiting for her, I saw that the Fire Brigade was busy pumping floodwater out of residents' basements.

The thing I remember most about 1959 was the glorious summer that we had that year. We decided that we would like to see something of South Devon that year. So some friends of ours, a Mr. and Mrs. Harris, recommended to us a guesthouse in Torquay where they holidayed each year. The two Misses Godfrey owned this guesthouse. We managed to book two weeks holiday there commencing Saturday 3rd June. We had had a glorious May and it was a beautiful fresh morning when we set out from my home on my scooter. We travelled via Croydon, Sutton, Epsom, Leatherhead and Guildford, then on to the Hog's Back and when we reached the end of it, we took the road to Winchester. We continued along the A31 through the New Forest until we reached Wimborne. We then noticed that the sky was becoming more and more cloudy. In due course we came to a signpost which read 'Dorchester – 7½ miles'. At that point we felt the first spots of rain. The rain grew steadily worse and we then came to another signpost which read 'Dorchester 1½ miles' by this time it was raining torrentially and just after that the engine stopped, for the same reason as it had at Ashtead the previous year. There was nothing for it but to push the scooter into Dorchester and we arrived in the town drenched. We thought that it would be another endlessly sunny day, so neither had worn any waterproof clothing, except for the leather jacket, which I was wearing. Brenda visited a store in the town and bought a complete set of clothing and a mac. Fortunately, the shop had a changing room. We put the wet clothing in a grip which was strapped to a luggage-rack behind the pillion. In my case, it was just my trousers that were saturated. So, I went into a shop, which sold fishing, camping equipment etc. and asked them if they had a pair of mackintosh trousers. They said that there were none in stock, and the best thing that they could offer me was a pair of fisherman's waders. I did not think much of this, but I had packed some scout shorts in my grip, so I would have to put those on and put the waders over the top of them. "I'm going to look jim-jammy in this get-up" I thought. But then I thought "It won't be so bad, it has stopped raining now; I'll now be able to start the scooter and not get off it again until we arrive at the Guest House in Torquay". But the darned thing wouldn't start. So I pushed it to Dorchester West Station and asked the booking clerk if one could get to Torquay. "Yes" he replied "but the journey will take 4¼ hours and you will have to change at Yeovil Pen Mill then Taunton and then Newton Abbot. The next train does not arrive here from Weymouth until 4.45p.m.

There was nothing for it but to wait until then and when the train arrived, we were told to put the scooter in the Guard's Van. I felt embarrassed by my appearance, wearing my scout shorts with waders over the top of them and hoped that we would be able to travel in empty carriages. But there was no hope of that!

When the train arrived at Yeovil Pen Mill station, we were told to get out. "What about our scooter?" I asked the guard.

"That stays on the train," he said. Then, to our dismay the train started to pull out of the station. However, to our great relief, it reversed into another platform. We were then told to get into the train again and then we were on our way to Taunton. There we were told to take the scooter out and we awaited the arrival of an express service, which would take us to Newton Abbot. Arriving there, we got out, took the scooter out of the van and awaited a train for Torquay. Finally, we took the scooter out of the van for the last time, pushed it through the concourse at Torquay station and then, joy of joys, I was able to start it up. Next, I got out a map of Torquay, which I had purchased earlier and soon found my way to the guesthouse. We apologised profusely to the Misses Godfrey for our late arrival and explained what had happened. They provided us with a lovely meal and told us not to worry. We then stopped up for a little while to let our dinner go down and then, thankfully, went to bed after a tiring day.

We awoke next morning to the sound of pouring rain, which continued all day, although we managed to shelter from it by going to the cinema in the afternoon. We then returned to the guest house for dinner and then watched television in the lounge as it was too wet to go out. It was still raining when we awoke the next day, so after breakfast, we decided to take shelter in some of the shops and stores in Torquay. When we were coming out of Woolworths, around midday, a really hot sun was emerging from behind the clouds. The afternoon was so hot, that we spent it on the beach and, thereafter, the weather was perfect for the rest of the holiday.

I can only remember that the start of our holiday produced the only sustained heavy rain during the whole of the summer that year. The weather was so good after our holiday, that I went to work on my temperamental old scooter for two months and until my next short holiday, towards the end of August. I worked in Lombard Street and used to park my scooter on a bombsite near Cannon Street station.

As I had reached the age of 25 that year, the Bank awarded me another three days holiday. They allowed me to add on another day's holiday as I was on holiday in Torquay on Whit-Monday, so I was able to go to summer camp with the Troop in August for four days. The camp was held that year at Charmouth, on the same farm as we had camped in 1949 and 1950; indeed camping in the same field as in 1949. The weather was perfect throughout and we went swimming from the beach at nearby Charmouth each day.

That year, we had a glorious Indian summer, which lasted until the end of October.

Babbacombe Downs, 1961.

Chapter Ten

RELATIVELY QUIET ON THE WEATHER FRONT, BUT A TIME OF CHANGE ON A PERSONAL FRONT

From the end of the glorious summer and Indian summer of 1959, there was not much remarkable weather until the bitterly cold winter of 1962-63. There were one or two days in the summers, when it was very hot and there was snow over the New Year period of 1961-62, which prevented Brenda and I attending a New Year's Eve dance at Beckenham, Kent, but I cannot remember much else to write about with regard to the weather.

It was, however, an important time for me with regard to my personal life. Brenda and I had got on so well during our fortnight's holiday in Torquay, that we got engaged immediately afterwards. We spent a fortnight's holiday at Torquay at the beginning of June 1960, staying again with the Misses Godfrey. Thankfully, we did not have the problems with the scooter, which we had had the previous year. This time, we decided to make an overnight stop and coming across a guesthouse in the pretty village of Charmouth with a 'Vacancies' sign in the window, we spent the night there.

The next day we had to cover the relatively short distance of about 50-miles to Torquay, but the weather was generally miserable, compared to the glorious weather we had had the previous year (apart from the first three days!).

The previous year, we had gone swimming nearly every day, but that year, I do not recall going in the water once, A lovely day had been predicted, however, for the day we were due to return home. So, I said to Brenda, "Let's go swimming before we go home. We are going to stop somewhere en route overnight, so we'll have time".

When the next day dawned, however, there was a thick sea mist, which did not look like clearing up. So, I said, "Let's get off as soon as we can. The mist will probably clear later. We'll see what it's like at Charmouth, as we have to pass through the village". When we reached Charmouth, however, the mist was almost as bad, so I rode on to the coastal village of West Bay, near Bridport. It was just the same there.

Undaunted, I took the Weymouth road via Abbotsbury. When we arrived there, we were met by a perfect sunny afternoon and we had a swim in the lovely clear water at Weymouth. We left Weymouth in the late afternoon and then had a lovely drive through the countryside, through the villages of Wool and Bere Regis and then through the town of Wimborne, before finally staying the night at an inn near Ringwood. We completed our journey home the next day.

It is strange, but apart from 1952, all the lovely summers that I could remember up to that time, were all odd-number years i.e. 1947, 1949, 1955, 1957 and 1959. I can recall that the rather miserable summers occurred in the even years i.e. 1948, 1950, 1956 and 1958, the exception being 1953.

I do not remember much remarkable weather in 1961, apart from an unseasonably hot fortnight in March; a Saturday at the beginning of July, when the temperature reached 91degF and heavy snow over the New Year period.

Brenda and I were married in the lovely old Church at Meopham. It was a perfect day for a wedding and Brenda looked lovely in her bridal gown. She held a bouquet of salmon-coloured roses and the four bridesmaids wore dresses of a similar colour. The day was sunny and warm, but not too hot, with just a light breeze.

After the reception, a friend of ours drove us to London, where we spent our wedding night at a hotel in the Bloomsbury area.

We had to get up early the next morning, as we had to get a taxi to take us to Paddington to catch the Cornish Riviera Express. We had reserved seats and our luggage had been sent on in advance to the hotel in Babbacombe where we were spending our honeymoon. We had to get out at Newton Abbot and wait for a train for Torquay and from there, we took a taxi to our hotel at nearby Babbacombe.

I cannot now recall the name of the hotel at which we stopped, but we enjoyed our stay there. The food was good and we had all the privacy we needed. We walked a lot, went swimming at the nearby beach and visited the shops in Torquay.

But, all too soon, we had to return from our honeymoon. We left Torquay on Thursday 22nd June for Rochester, Kent as we were moving into our brand-new home at nearby Chattenden the next day. We spent the night at the Gordon Hotel, Rochester, which we found to be an old-fashioned and rather sinister place. Our room was accessed through a side door, halfway up a staircase. In the room, was a small marble-topped table, on which stood a large bowl and jug for the purpose of washing. Soap and towels were, of course, provided, as was hot water each morning . Still, the bed was quite comfortable and the food was alright. Nevertheless, we were glad to be on our way the next morning.

We took a taxi to our new dwelling at Chattenden, where we met a representative from the builders, who handed us the keys. As far as I can remember, payment to the builders had been organised in advance a week before our wedding. Now, we had bought most of our large furniture from a shop by the name of Hardys of Chatham and their lorry arrived at our house shortly afterwards. At around the same time, Brenda's father arrived in his van, with many other household goods and also, our wedding presents. We worked hard that day moving in, but we could not have managed without the help of Brenda's parents. We could not do any work the following day, as we had to go to the wedding of my Scouting friend, Ron S and his fiancée Pat. The wedding was held at St. Michael and All Angel's Church, Sydenham and the reception was held at a restaurant in nearby Downham, not far from where Pat lived.

I had a scare on the following Saturday 1st July. We had a sudden heatwave that day, with the temperature reaching 91degF. I had to go to work that morning, but Brenda, as agreed by the bank, no longer had to work on Saturday mornings. Before I set off for work, Brenda told me that she was going into Chatham to buy some more things for the home, including some stair-rods. I was lucky insofar as banks in the City of London closed at 11.30-a.m. instead of 12-noon. This was because of the 'Town Clearing'.

At that time, I worked for New Issues and Registrars Department and as we were strictly a non-banking department, I either got away at 11.30 or just after. It was very hot travelling down in the stuffy train, but I was looking forward to my lunch, as Brenda said that she would be home in good time to prepare it. I arrived home at around 1.15 in the afternoon and after opening the door, I called out to Brenda. But there was no answer. 'The shopping must have taken her longer than she thought and she will be home soon', I thought to myself.

I waited and waited, but she did not arrive and by two-o'clock, I was in a state of panic, I had no means of contacting her (no mobile phones in those days!). Also, we were not on the phone, so she could not make contact. So, I walked out to the bus stop on the Isle of Grain road and waited in the blazing heat. There were buses about every 20 minutes and one came and went. But, thankfully Brenda arrived on the next bus. I remember that she was carrying a very heavy grip full of stair-rods and she had come over faint in the blazing heat in Chatham She told me that a kindly shopkeeper had given her a drink and made her rest in his shop until she felt better. Was I relieved to see her!

We were settling down well to married life and everything was going smoothly, but one thing, however, made me feel a little sad. Brenda quite rightly suggested that it was high time that I got rid of my decrepit old scooter and bought a brand-new one, as we now relied on the scooter to get us to Strood station every morning to catch the 7.38-a.m train to Cannon Street. She said that the management would not think much of us if we were frequently late, because heavy rain had got into the carburettor and stopped the engine on the way to Strood station. I had become attached to my temperamental old Lambretta; I had travelled some distances on it and had, at times, some unforgettable adventures with it. Still, I could see the sense in what my wife was saying, so reluctantly, I took it along to a scooter-dealer near Chatham station and traded it in for a brand new one. I felt sad when I left my old scooter with the dealer, but I did see it one more time. We often used to walk from our estate down a steep footpath to Upnor, a lovely little village on the banks of the River Medway. One day, we walked down there and suddenly I spied my old scooter outside a house in Upnor. So, it had either been bought by a resident of Upnor, or by someone who was visiting. I still remember the old registration: PYP 178.

We still intended to go to cricket club dances in Beckenham after we were married and we attended the end of season dance at the beginning of October. We both agreed that it was one of the best ones that we had attended and we were very much looking forward to the one on New Year's Eve.

Unfortunately, it started to snow heavily on the morning of New Year's Eve and did not let up all day. We had heard on the radio that snow was making it difficult to get to London by road or rail, so at about four-o'clock in the afternoon, we decided to ring Mum to tell her that we wouldn't be coming. We walked to the telephone box in the Isle of Grain road and told Mum of our decision. As we were walking back to our house, we bumped into two of our neighbours, Alan and Yvonne. "Are you doing anything tonight?", they asked.

"We were", we replied, "But, we have had to cancel going to a New Year's Eve Dance in Beckenham, because of the weather".

"Why don't you spend New Year's Eve with us," they said, "We had not planned anything special for tonight". We accepted their offer gratefully and we had an enjoyable evening and saw in the New Year with them. We had no more snow that night and I managed to get to work the next morning.

I don't recall any remarkable weather in this country in 1962 until December, but we had a fierce storm and a heatwave during our holiday in June in Switzerland.

We had booked a coach trip to a village by the name of Weggis on Lake Lucerne, where we were to spend a week's holiday. The coach took us to Dover, where we caught a ferry to Ostend. Then, we drove through Belgium to Namur, where we stopped overnight at a hotel. The coach then went on to Metz in Germany, where we had another stop, before finally arriving at our hotel in Weggis. The scenery in Switzerland was breathtaking. We spent quite a lot of time walking in and around Weggis and we also visited a beer cellar in Lucerne on a couple of nights and on the Saturday went to an open-air theatre overlooking Lake Lucerne. It was hot that day, but the following day, the temperature was going to climb to 100degF. We went to see a colourful street procession threading its way through the streets of Weggis, but it was so hot, that we did not watch it for long, but retreated to the air-conditioned comfort of our hotel, We noticed that most of the other people in our party were doing the same thing. For me, the highlight of the week was a coach trip to Interlaken, where I thought the scenery was breathtaking.

We would go swimming in Lake Lucerne and I would swim out to a diving platform, which was moored in the lake and then back. One night, we had a fierce storm and the gale-force winds caused most of these platforms to break free of their moorings and they were seen floating down Lake Lucerne. There were also branches of trees floating in the lake.

Fortunately, the fierce heat of the Sunday did not last and it was quite comfortable by the Thursday when we had to go home. As on the journey outwards, we had two overnight stops; at Pirmasens in Germany and in Brussels, the latter, in a really luxurious hotel. We arrived in London quite late on Saturday night at around 10-p.m. and stopped the night with my parents.

The weather during the rest of the summer and early autumn of 1962 was unremarkable, but things were soon to change!

The frozen River Medway at Rochester, January 1963.

Chapter Eleven

THE WINTER OF 1962-63

The big freeze of 1962-63 started on Boxing Day, but I sensed that we were in for a bad winter before then. There was some heavy snow in November and at the beginning of December, there was a week of freezing fog. I remember that week well.

On the first Monday in December, I was due to start a new job in the Securities Department of the bank in Lombard Street, having been transferred there from the bank's New Issue and Registrars Department in Gresham Street. Due to the freezing fog, the trains from Strood were arriving at Cannon Street roughly an hour late each day and my new departmental boss was not impressed by my being late each morning. The freezing fog, of course, became much worse after dark.

Now, our estate was populated by young married couples, many of whom owned cars. Most of the chaps used to catch the 7.38 a.m. train to

Cannon Street, as we did. Now, Brenda did not want me to use the scooter in the winter, after slithering about on the ice during the cold snap in November one morning, trying to get to Strood station. There were four neighbours who used to use their cars to get to and from the station - Joe, Michael, Brian and Alan. There were usually two cars in use and Brenda and I made sure that our neighbours were adequately reimbursed for their petrol and their trouble. Lifts at night were more difficult, as we did not always catch the same train and Brenda finished at 3 p.m. anyway, apart from Fridays.

One night during that week, however, I got out at Strood station and Brian was on the train, with, I think, Michael and Joe. Brian was the only one who had his car in the station car park and he offered us a lift home. Brian drove off and the fog was really bad and once we had driven out of the lit-up area, it was almost impossible to see anything. So, Brian asked for a volunteer to walk along the side of the road with a torch. Of course, I volunteered for the job! The fog was so bad that I could scarcely see Brian's car, which was crawling along about 2-3 yards away from me. After what seemed like an endless walk in the freezing fog, we finally arrived at the top of Lodge Hill and turned right into the estate. We were all thankful to arrive home in one piece.

Mum and Dad had invited us to Sydenham on Boxing Day to celebrate Geoff's birthday. It was a very cold day and I did not fancy travelling up to Sydenham on the scooter and as we were staying overnight, I did not fancy leaving it in the car park at Strood station. So, we decided to catch a bus from the main road, just outside the estate, which would take us to about 1/4-mile from Strood station. When we arrived at the bus stop I felt in my pockets to see whether I had what I needed, then, to my dismay, I discovered that I had left my glasses at home, which meant that I would not be able to read or watch television very well.

I, therefore, suggested that Brenda went down by bus and that I would race home, pick up my glasses and come down by scooter. I met Brenda at the station and when I arrived there, my hands were numb with the cold. I could sense even then that we were in for some exceptionally cold weather. I pushed the scooter under the station subway with my frozen hands and left it just outside the station building.

After we arrived at my parents' house, it started to snow heavily and continued to snow every day for well over a week. Boxing Day was on a weekday that year, so we had to go to work the next morning. We trudged up to Lower Sydenham station in the deep snow and somehow managed to get to work. The next day, which was a Friday, we had to travel up from Strood.

It snowed very heavily that weekend and on the Sunday morning, I tried to open the front door to get in the milk, but I couldn't open it because of the depth of the snow. Fortunately, I was able to open the back door and go round the side of the house to get the milk in. After that, I furiously shovelled snow away from our front door, so that we might get out. It snowed hard the following week, with temperatures well below freezing. Our train arrived at Cannon Street every day, but it used to arrive anything up to an hour late, which was not surprising in the awful conditions. Our bosses were tolerant over our lateness, because most of us, including some of the management, were in the same boat.

As mentioned previously, we returned to Strood on the Thursday evening (the day after Boxing Day) and saw my scooter standing forlornly outside Strood station in about a foot of snow. It would have been impossible to even think of moving it and riding it home, so it would just have to stay there until there was a thaw. On Saturday 5th January, we had a slight respite from the snow and as I had to work every other Saturday in the Securities Department, I was working on that particular Saturday. After work, I was waiting at London Bridge station for my train, when I bumped into one of my neighbours, a chap by the name of Les. He was a handsome chap and bore a strong resemblance to Errol Flynn.

When we were on the train, I mentioned to Les that I had been unable to use my scooter since Boxing Day, as it had been laid up at Strood station in over a foot of snow. "Look, Michael", he said, "There has not been any more snow today and conditions have improved slightly, so I will help you to push it out of the station concourse, then under the subway. The road outside the station has been gritted and so has the Isle of Grain road, the only difficulty that we should have, is pushing the scooter through the deep snow round the estate".

Once we arrived at the station, Les and I managed to push the scooter out of the station concourse, then through the subway and on to Station Road. Thereupon, Les mounted the pillion and we rode off. We had no difficulties until we arrived at our estate, the snow was nine-inches to a foot deep. Les was a strong chap, but it was as much as we could do to push the scooter through the deep snow to my house. I thanked Les for his help and then he walked the short distance to his house.

The bitter weather did not let up at all the following week, in fact, it became colder. I think that the temperature in London on 8th January was 8degF and temperatures were well below freezing on most days. The winter of 1962-63 seemed worse to me than the one in 1947, but I am sure that it was only because the former was more recent than the latter.

I am pretty sure that there was more snow in 1947, but I cannot remember so many inches of tightly packed ice on the pavements as there were in 1962-63. Strangely enough, my parents lived in a built-up area and the ice seemed even thicker there than at Chattenden. We had plenty of snow too and when I was walking on the estate, it often came over the tops of my Wellington boots. I could go on and on about that winter, but I will only recount two more tales about it.

The coldest day that I can remember that winter was Sunday January 13th. The windows in the house were crystallized with frost and so were the windows of the train we were travelling on between Rochester and Meopham, on the way to visiting Brenda's parents. I managed to peer through the frost-encrusted windows of the train and saw people skiing on the steep hills around the village of Sole Street. When I visited Brenda's parents on a Sunday, her father used to give me two or three bottles of beer to drink before we went home. There were not many fridges in those days and her father used to keep the beer in a cool place in the house. That night the beer was as cold as if it had come straight out of a freezer.

The bitterly cold weather did not let up at all during the next week and it was bitterly cold at night as well. We did not have central heating in those days, just a boiler in the kitchen and an open fire in the lounge. Brenda and I used to sit in the lounge with our overcoats on watching the television, but still we were cold.

I think it must have been just as cold on 23rd and 24th January as on 13th, as on those days, parts of the nearby River Medway froze over. For some reason, which I cannot now remember, I had a couple of day's holiday booked. Brenda had to go to work and on the first morning, I discovered that I wanted something from the local shop. So, I trudged through the snow to the shop, which was on the main road, made my purchase and returned home. When I reached the door, I felt in my pockets for my front door key, but to my dismay I couldn't find it. I then realised that I had left it on the kitchen table.

I was in a state of panic. Brenda wouldn't be home until 4.30 p.m. at the earliest. I couldn't shelter in a neighbour's house, as everybody was at work. 'What was I to do?', I thought. I then noticed that the garage had not been locked, so there was no other option but to shelter in there. However, the freezing garage would have been just as cold as standing outside. Then an idea came to me.

The ladders were in the garage and I recalled that we had a most unusual type of soft putty in our windows - it was like plasticine! So, I took the ladder round to the back of the house. 'Kitchen, no good', I thought. There is one really large pane of glass, which will surely crack in the bitter cold and a very small window which I will never be able to climb through'. I then looked upstairs to the back bedroom. There was a large pane of glass and a smaller one. 'If I take the putty out with a knife (which fortunately was also in the garage), I can climb through". I had heard on the radio earlier, that parts of the Medway had frozen up and I thought, 'Just my luck. I am stuck out here on a ladder, on a day that is cold enough to freeze the Medway'!

Anyway, I succeeded in removing the pane of glass, climbed into the bedroom and retrieved my keys. I then had to climb up the ladder to put back the pane of glass. Brenda could scarcely believe what had happened when she came home.

There was no let-up in the freezing conditions during the rest of the month and through the whole of February. This endless big freeze was really getting us down, as well as everybody else, I should imagine. As we went to bed on the night of Friday 1st March, I thought to myself, 'At least I won't have to get up early in this weather', as it was my Saturday off. We awoke the next morning to the sound of drip, drip, drip and it felt warmer. The snow was melting and water was dripping off our roof. I could have jumped for joy, as the long-awaited thaw was here at last!

Picture taken of Venice, July 1966.

Chapter Twelve

THE MID-SIXTIES

I do not wish to bore the reader by writing too much about unremarkable weather. I cannot think of much extraordinary weather which occurred between the bitterly cold winter of 1962-63 and the terrible floods in South London and Kent in September 1968.

Therefore, in order to give my story some continuity, as well as writing about the weather during this period, I have written about some events in my personal life including holidays taken between 1963 and 1968.

Unlike 1947, a glorious summer did not follow the awful winter in 1963. That year, we went on holiday in July and stayed at a hotel in Mawgan Porth, a coastal village near Newquay. We were going to travel down by scooter, but on the Saturday, we awoke to the sound of torrential rain. This showed no sign of stopping, so we decided that we were not going to travel around 300 miles on the scooter in such bad weather. I had considered the possibility of bad weather and had found out that one could get to Padstow direct from Waterloo. I cannot now remember exactly when the train was scheduled to leave for Padstow, but I think that it was somewhere around 10-a.m. We were able to travel direct from Strood station to Waterloo East and then we walked over a footbridge to the mainline station. Our main luggage had been sent on in advance.

I think that the journey took around six hours. It would have been a lovely journey on a nice day, but we could hardly see out of the train windows, because of the torrential rain.

When we arrived at Padstow, we walked out on to the rainswept station concourse, hoping that there might be a taxi around to take us to our hotel at Mawgan Porth. Suddenly a most sinister-looking man approached us and asked us if we needed a taxi. I hesitated for a moment and then I said, "Yes", because, although I did not like the look of this man, there were no other taxis about. He pointed to a dilapidated old black car, on which there was no indication that it was a taxi and we got in. It was not long, however, before we reached our hotel, so I thanked him and gave him a tip. The receptionist showed us to our room and it was so cold and damp, that the first thing we did was to switch on the electric fire. The rain did not stop for the rest of the day.

Now, a very strange thing happened on the day before my holiday. At that time, I worked for Securities Department of the bank. Opposite me worked a chap by the name of Brian, who worked in the Loans Department. I had known him some 11- years earlier, when he came to the Edgware Road branch of the bank to take over from me as the junior clerk, after I had reported for National Service and I had spent a short time teaching him the job.

That Friday afternoon, I told him that Brenda and I were going on a fortnight's holiday to Mawgan Porth in Cornwall. "Good heavens" he said, "My girlfriend - Rose - and I are going on holiday tomorrow and we are staying on a farm about 15-miles away from where you will be. We're travelling down by car. How are you getting there?".

"By scooter," I said (because I thought that we were at that time). Brian asked me for the name of the hotel and asked us if he and his girlfriend could meet us there on the Monday morning? I phoned Brenda, who worked in another department, told her the amazing news and asked if she was agreeable to the meeting. So, we met Brian and Rose, whom we had never seen before, at our hotel on the Monday at around 10-a.m. I told Brian that we had abandoned the idea of travelling down by scooter, in view of the appalling weather and had travelled down by train. "We'll take you out every other day in the car, if you're agreeable", said Brian.

We thought it was very kind of them and gladly accepted their kind offer. We visited quite a few places in the car, including Padstow, Port Isaac, Looe, Polperro and St. Ives (twice). The weather was generally miserable, except for one of the trips to St. Ives, when we had quite a nice day. Of all the places we visited, St. Ives was our favourite. On the days that we didn't go out with Brian and Rose, we usually went to Newquay by bus. I thought that it was a most over-rated place, but the fact that the weather was always miserable when we went, might have influenced my opinion. We only had one really gorgeous day during the whole fortnight and that was the middle Sunday, when Brian and Rose visited us at Mawgan Porth. We spent the whole day on the beach and we had had an enjoyable holiday, in spite of a lot of bad weather. One thing we noticed in our travels, was that many of the numerous palm trees in Cornwall were brown and withered, as a result of the terrible winter.

1964 was an uneventful year for weather, as I recall, so I will not bore the reader by writing about it. The summer was generally pleasant without being really hot.

On 23rd January 1965, we moved from our house at Chattenden to one at Borough Green, a village not far from Sevenoaks, Kent. The main reason for our moving, was that Brenda was experiencing great difficulty in travelling. She had agreed reduced hours with the Bank and she was allowed to leave at 3-p.m. every day, with the exception of Friday, when she worked until 6-p.m. So, four days a week she used to catch a train from Cannon Street station, which was non-stop to Chatham, but then her troubles began. There was very heavy traffic in the Medway towns, including many heavy lorries because, until some time in 1964 when a new bridge was built across the Medway at Cuxton, there was no way of bypassing the Medway towns. The traffic through the towns was frequently gridlocked and Brenda was getting home not much earlier than me. I often used to leave at 5-p.m., catch the 5.18 train from Cannon Street, which was non-stop to Rochester and almost immediately catching another train for the mile or so journey back to Strood, thus avoiding all the traffic problems of the Medway towns. On most days, at Strood station, I would jump on my scooter and be home within 10-minutes. The situation in the Medway towns, the fortnight before Christmas, was so bad that I used to arrive home before Brenda very often. The building of the new bridge over the Medway in 1964 did not help much, until well after we had moved to Borough Green, as nobody had thought to build a transport cafe on the by-pass and most lorry-drivers refused to use the bridge until one was built. Clearly this situation could not go on for Brenda, so in January 1965, we moved to Borough Green, which had excellent links to Victoria, Holborn and Blackfriars stations and we only had a 10-minute walk to Borough Green station.

The day we moved house was a very cold day. We used a removal firm called Rings of Rochester and I remember that their vans had a big picture of Rochester Castle on each side. We had no car at the time and the removal men kindly let us travel in their van. We even joined them for a slap-up breakfast in a transport cafe in Strood, before travelling to our new home in Borough Green.

The removal men parked their van in front of our new house. There was a steep slope down to our front door and this slope was very icy and the men slid large items, such as the gas-cooker and the washing machine, down the slope. We worked really hard that day and again we could not have managed without the help of Brenda's parents.

The local shop was situated opposite the Borough Green recreation ground, which was about a 10-minute walk away from our house and during the afternoon, I walked down through the snow and ice to get some essential provisions.

The day after we moved, Sir Winston Churchill died and on the next day, when I went to work I noticed that the Union Jack in the recreation ground was flying at half-mast, as were all other flags as a mark of respect for, perhaps, one of the greatest men who had ever lived.

The summer of 1965 was pleasant for most of the time as I recall, without being too hot. Brenda and I spent a week in July at the Cliff-tops Hotel at Shanklin on the Isle of Wight. It was a lovely hotel, but we had rather strange weather. For most of the time there was a sea mist, which the sun was trying hard to penetrate. One day at the beginning of the week, we sat out in the sun for rather a long time. The next day, Brenda woke up and found it difficult to see. She had sunburn on the skin around her eyes, which were just slits. I immediately took her to Casualty Department at a hospital in Shanklin and, to our amazement, there were many other people there with the same problem. The doctor told us that a misty sun is particularly dangerous and that Brenda should remain indoors until the swelling had gone down and after that, not to sit in the sun.

My father had been badly sunburned by a misty sun when on holiday in Weymouth in 1953. Dad and I had taken a boat out to sea for an hour and despite Dad keeping his vest on throughout, he still had to have the doctor in the next day. This was a Monday and the Doctor told him to stay in bed for two days. The first week in October was exceptionally hot for that time of the year and we were lucky enough to have been on holiday that week, visiting some of the local beauty spots.

I do not have much to report on the weather in Great Britain in 1966.

That year we spent a fortnight's holiday in Lido di Jesolo, near Venice. Much against our better judgement, we decided to travel by overnight coach. The coach took us to Folkestone and then we caught a ferry to Ostend. The coach did not stop on its journey from Ostend to Lido di Jesolo, except for meals and for tea or coffee breaks. In the middle of the night, we were travelling on a German Autobahn. I slept for the most of the journey, but at one point, woke up to find my wife very worried. "I'm sure that the driver is going to fall asleep any minute. He keeps trying to nod off", she said, "I am going to wake up the relief driver". With that, she tapped the relief driver on the shoulder and told him her fears, whereupon he got up and told the driver to pull in to the side of the autobahn and to let him take over. The old driver sat down on a seat in the coach and immediately fell asleep. About a week after we returned from our holiday, we learned that there had been a coach crash with fatalities on the same stretch of autobahn, the cause of which was thought to be driver fatigue. We felt stiff and uncomfortable trying to sleep sitting-up in our seats and what with our worries about safety, vowed that this would be the first and last time that we would travel this way.

The weather during our first week at Lido di Jesolo was perfect and we spent every day on the beach, apart from one day when we went to Venice by coach and spent the nights mingling with the crowds in the balmy night air, looking in the shops and eating pizzas and drinking coffee. We very much enjoyed our day in Venice. We visited St. Mark's Cathedral and the Doge's Palace, had a coffee in St. Mark's Square, and then in the afternoon, went on a ride in a gondola. I paid the gondolier up front, and we set off. Also on board was a singer, a burly man and like many Italians, he had a good voice and serenaded us. It was a once in a lifetime's experience and when we returned to the quay, I gave the gondolier a tip for his services and for those of the singer. When we got out of the gondola, however, the singer ran after us saying, "You lika the singing?, You lika the singing?". He kept saying this and then the penny dropped. He wanted a separate tip. As he was becoming more menacing, I gave him a tip and we walked back to St. Marks Square, where we were to meet the other passengers.

The weather during our second week, however, was generally poor. We had another excursion planned for that week, a visit to the Venetian Islands of Murano, Burano and Torcello. We had a particularly bad day for this outing, in fact the weather was reminiscent of a November day in England. As we were travelling towards Venice, it was raining torrentially and the coach driver quipped, "We shall soon be crossing the River Piave, unless the Piave crosses us first". Thankfully, the rain had eased off when we reached Venice, where we caught a boat to the Venetian Islands. First, we visited the island of Murano, where we watched the glass-blowers at work manufacturing the famous Venetian glass. We bought several pieces of glassware there, some to give as presents and some for ourselves. We then went on to Burano where we had a meal. I cannot now remember whether we visited Torcello.

We were in Italy during the second half of July and we noticed many gloomy Italian faces in the bars and cafes, as Italy, one of the hot favourites to win the World Cup, had made an early exit from the competition.

We had enjoyed our holiday, apart from the coach travel and we returned home just in time to see England win the World Cup, beating West Germany in the Final by 4 goals to two.

In March 1967, our son, David, was born. I thought that Brenda needed a holiday and although David was only three months old, we decided to spend a week in a caravan in June at Holland-on-Sea, a coastal village near Clacton. We thought that we would have everything at hand for David's needs, we could do as we liked and would not be worried about keeping other people awake, The weather that week was lovely throughout, without being too hot. We spent nearly every day in the open, sitting on the grass verges near the sea, with David in his carrycot. One day, however, we visited Brenda's aunt and uncle in their bungalow at nearby Jaywick. They were telling us about their hair-raising experience on the night of 31st January 1953, when high seas flooded much of the East coast; they had to sit on the roof of their bungalow for hours, before being rescued by boat (I have written about the East Coast floods in a previous chapter).

We had enjoyed our week's holiday and wanted to book a caravan on the same site the following year, but I felt that the travelling arrangements would have to be different. We had had to travel to Victoria by train, then take a taxi to Liverpool Street station, then catch a train to Clacton and then take a taxi to the caravan site at Holland-on-Sea. I felt that we had had too much luggage to cope with, what with David's carrycot on wheels and our heavy luggage. The travelling difficulties were similar on the journey home.

So, the following June, my father took us all the way to Holland-on-Sea in his large Ford Zephyr. Mum and Dad stayed overnight in the caravan and went home the next day. Unfortunately, the weather during that week was totally opposite to the weather we had experienced the previous year. It was wet and cold and the flimsy walls of the caravan were insufficient to keep out the cold at night. Also, the previous year, it had been very quiet at night, but this time there were a lot of rowdy youngsters staying in some of the caravans and they seemed to be making a din at all hours. Therefore, we were not sorry to go home and vowed that we would never stay in a caravan again. On the homeward journey, we caught a coach from Clacton to Gravesend, where Brenda's father met us and took us home in his car.

If we thought that our holiday weather had been generally wet, it was nothing to what we were to experience in the coming September!

Seal Hollow Road, Sevenoaks. Conditions were similar in Ightham.
By courtesy of Sevenoaks Chronicle.

Chapter Thirteen

THE IGHTHAM RAPIDS

On Saturday 15th September 1968, it rained hard all day. I went for a walk in the evening when the rain had finally stopped, but I still thought the sky looked stormy and menacing. That night 4½ inches of rain fell on the nearby town of West Malling (I later discovered from a newspaper that it had been the wettest place in Great Britain) and it was still raining torrentially the next morning.

We were going to visit my parents in Sydenham and had planned to walk to Borough Green station with David in the pushchair. We had then planned to catch a train to Bromley South and then another one to Beckenham Hill and from there, walk about a mile to my parent's house. However, when I looked out the window, I had never seen rain like it! So, walking to the station was absolutely out of the question and I rang up a local taxi driver by the name of Mr. Kennett and asked him if he would take us to the station.

On the way down, we noticed that there was already some flooding in Borough Green, with some low-lying properties badly affected. When we arrived at the station, there was a big notice at the front of the entrance hall saying that due to landslides caused by flooding, no trains were running. I asked Mr. Kennett whether he would mind waiting while I popped in to see the booking clerk? I asked the latter if trains were running on the main line from Sevenoaks to London and his reply was, "They are at the moment".

I knew the times of the buses from the bus garage to Sevenoaks and the times of the trains from there to London and I figured I could get to Lewisham by changing *en route*. With that, I telephoned my father and told him what had happened and asked him if he would mind picking us up from Lewisham station at around one-o'clock. With that, I then asked Mr. Kennett to take us to the bus station.

Although the bus for Sevenoaks left on time, I remember being rather worried by the amount of water there was about on the roads and whether I had made the right decision by trying to get to Lewisham at all? About a mile out of Borough Green, the driver had to turn left towards the village of Ightham and as we were travelling along, I noticed little waves of water coming towards us. As we got nearer to the village centre, these gentle waves turned to rapids, as one might see in a Western movie.

With that, the driver decided to stop. There was a small factory by the name of 'Faithfulls' to the right of us, which was on higher ground, so the driver turned his big double-decker bus into the factory car-park. He then got out and had a chat with his conductor about whether they should go on to Sevenoaks or return to the bus garage? Anyway, they decided to continue the journey and the driver climbed inside his cab and started to move forward out of the car park. He then attempted to turn right towards the village centre, when, suddenly, the 'rapids' took control of the bus. It careered across the road, demolishing a front-gate and it was only the volume of water which stopped us crashing into the house.

With David, who was only aged 18-months, sat on Brenda's lap, we were sitting on one of the downstairs rear seats (the pushchair had been stowed in the luggage space at the front of the bus). Suddenly, some bright spark opened the rear emergency door without making sure that the exit door at the front of the bus was also open. The 'rapids' rushed in and I thought that we were all going to be drowned.

With that, the driver raced round to open the exit-door at the front of the bus and the water rushed out again. The driver told us all to remain in our seats and before long, a tractor appeared and ferried the passengers, one-by-one, across the rapids. After about half-an-hour, a small Maidstone & District single-decker arrived to take the passengers back to the bus station.

Apparently, the police had insisted on a small bus, as they were worried about possible road subsidence beneath the floodwater. Once we arrived at the bus station, we then had to walk the short distance to our home, soaked to the skin.

The first thing I did when I arrived home was to phone my mother to tell her what had happened. It must have been about two in the afternoon and Mum said the flooding was very bad in Lower Sydenham as well and that Dad had not yet arrived home. I felt very worried and I kept ringing at regular intervals, until around 3 o'clock, when I was relieved to learn that he had arrived home safely.

Dad had obviously had a horrendous journey back from Lewisham station and he told me that he had given up on us when it was approaching two-o'clock and we still had not arrived. It was a wonder that he had even got out of Lewisham, as it was badly flooded around the Lewisham clock tower area, which had been caused by the nearby River Ravensbourne bursting its banks.

Dad had managed to drive along the road from Lewisham to Catford, but found it impossible to get to Sydenham, as the overflowing Rivers Ravensbourne and Pool had caused widespread flooding. The Ravensbourne flows by the side of Peter Pan's Boating Lake and people were using the boats to rescue some of their belongings from their flooded homes.

Somehow, Dad had managed to get to Beckenham, driving through the town, until he discovered a route to Sydenham, using Kent House Road, which wasn't closed. Dad had then driven along this road and then into Kent House Lane, where he encountered more bad flooding, although as he was driving through the floods, some large, submerged object, badly damaged the bodywork of his Ford Zephyr. Although he managed to reach home (at that point he only had about 1/2 mile to go), he had, of course, to drive the car to a garage the following week for extensive bodywork repairs.

The flooding was widespread in Kent and South East London and many towns and villages were flooded, particularly those which were near rivers. The River Medway burst its banks and Tonbridge in particular, was badly flooded, as was Maidstone, Yalding, East Peckham and many other places. There was a lot of serious flooding in Borough Green, although we were lucky, as we were on high ground. Despite this, the houses and the bungalow below us and near the railway line, were badly flooded. The general stores opposite the recreation ground were completely flooded, as were many other properties in the village.

In addition, there was also serious flooding in South-east London and Lower Sydenham, Catford, Bellingham and Lewisham were also badly affected, as were many other parts of the South-east.

As I had to go to work the next day, I rang up both Borough Green and Sevenoaks stations to try and clarify the transport situation and I was told that there were no trains running to London, because of landslides caused by the torrential rain. I then tried to catch a coach from the bus station to Victoria coach station. I knew that there should be a coach leaving at 7.40 a.m. and although I waited and waited, no coach turned up. No reason was given, but I think it was undoubtedly because of the widespread flooding in Kent.

Before I leave the subject of the September floods, I will just write about the hair-raising experience of one of my cousins and her husband on Sunday 16th. They lived in a downstairs maisonette at the Bellingham end of Worsley Bridge Road and just behind their back garden, ran the River Pool. The phenomenal amount of rain had caused the Pool to burst its banks and suddenly floodwater rushed into the maisonette, until it reached hip height, causing their furniture and carpets to be ruined and they had to make a hasty exit from their home. The flooding was very bad where my cousin lived and at a nearby railway bridge over Southend Lane, so much floodwater collected under that bridge, that one could see no light under the bridge.

There was a pillarbox at the end of Worsley Bridge Road and there was about 4-inches of it protruding out of the water. Because of these floods, my cousin and her husband had to move into temporary accommodation for some time until their insurance claim was settled and their home completely redecorated and refurbished. One way and another I was glad to see the back of 1968.

White Christmas 1970.

Chapter Fourteen

A WHITE CHRISTMAS

I cannot recall much remarkable weather in 1969, although we had quite a good summer without it being too hot. At the beginning of the year, we were in a quandary as to where to go for our summer holiday? We certainly did not want to spend it in a caravan again after our experience the previous year. We were talking about our dilemma to one of Brenda's friends, who had a son the same age as David and the question was posed, "Why don't we all go away together? How about trying Worthing, it is quite a nice resort?". So, we sent away for a brochure about Worthing and looked at the hotels, which were advertised as 'children-friendly'. We selected one and rang them up to see if they had any vacancies for a certain week in August. The proprietor said that they had, so we booked up for a week.

The weather was not too bad that week, but the hotel turned out to be most unfriendly to children. There were several permanent elderly residents there who were always grumbling about the noise that David and his friend were making. The head waiter had a drink problem and did not turn up for work in a fit state sometimes and one-day, I heard a blazing row between the proprietor and his wife. All in all, I was glad to get home from this holiday. One good thing was that I did not have to carry a lot of heavy luggage any great distance, as a Southdown coach took us from Borough Green bus station to the bus station at Worthing.

We had some very heavy snow in the first two weeks of March in 1970, but thankfully when we moved in to our house five years earlier, there was oil-fired central heating in place. However, we were finding this type of heating to be more and more expensive, so that month we changed over to gas central heating. I did not see the workmen at all, as I was at work. They arrived at the house one day at the beginning of March and Brenda let them in. That day they had just come to leave their materials with us, laying all their copper-piping on the back lawn.

That night, it snowed very heavily and this piping was covered by several inches of snow. I think that a different team of workmen must have turned up the next day, because finding no copper-piping they went out and came back with another lot. The snow and ice took at least a week to clear, but when the thaw came, all the copper piping was revealed on the lawn. I rang up the Gas Board about it who said they would send somebody to collect it.

In August of that year, we took David to a childrens' hotel in Boscombe. We sent for a brochure from the Bournemouth Tourist Office and booked a week in August at a 'children-friendly' hotel, situated in Owls Road, Boscombe. This time, the hotel was as advertised in the brochure and we enjoyed our stay there. The weather was generally good as I recall and we spent most days on Boscombe Beach, but one day we took David by bus to beautiful Poole Park. He enjoyed feeding the ducks, geese and other birds on the lakes and he enjoyed a ride round the lake on a little train.

However, as I found in 1967, I found the travelling a problem. We had to take a taxi to Borough Green station, then we caught a train to Victoria, then took another taxi to Waterloo, from there we travelled by train to Bournemouth and from there took a taxi to our hotel. We repeated this procedure, but in reverse on the day we went home. I decided that I must acquire some four- wheeled transport before we next went on our summer holiday, especially as there was going to be four of us soon.

Our daughter, Alison, was born in October. Like David, she was a lovely baby and we were very proud parents.

I had always wanted a white Christmas. I remember snow flurries on

Christmas night in 1956 and snow falling on Boxing Day in 1962, but I had never seen a Christmas card-type of white Christmas. But, in 1970 I got my wish.

As I recall, it started snowing heavily on Christmas Eve and by Christmas Day, the snow was quite deep. We were going to Brenda's parents for the day and about midday, her father collected us in his car. There was not usually much traffic about on Christmas Day and the roads were in a dangerous state with plenty of snow and ice about.

Brenda's mother cooked us an excellent dinner and as well as watching television in the afternoon, we also watched the snow coming down all the time. After we had had Christmas tea, Brenda's father said to us, "I will take you home now, because if this weather gets any worse, you won't get home at all". The weather was really bad, when he drove us home and we were worried about his getting home safely. About 30 minutes after he had left, we rang up and were relieved to learn that he had arrived home safely.

The weather was even worse the next day and there was more snow and ice about. We were supposed to be entertaining Brenda's parents, but early that Boxing Day morning, Brenda's father rang up to say that travelling was out of the question in such bad conditions.

The following day was a Saturday, so I did not have to go to work. We were supposed to be entertaining Brenda's brother, his wife and their two children. They lived at Snodland, a village less than 10 miles from us. Now, her brother was a very skilful driver, who would go out in conditions which would daunt others, but on this occasion, the conditions that day were even too bad for him to chance coming to see us.

At the beginning of 1971, we wrote to the hotel in Owls Road, Boscombe, asking if there was a vacancy for two adults and two children for a week in August? We did receive a reply, but it just stated that the hotel had closed down. We still had the brochure, so we wrote to a Mr. Fletcher, who was the proprietor of a 'children-friendly hotel' situated near Sea Road, Boscombe He wrote back saying that he had a vacancy for two adults and two children for a week in August.

I then tried to address the problem of transport. I held a full motor-cycle licence, which would enable me to drive a three-wheel vehicle without my having to drive with L plates and without my having to take a driving test. I could have chosen to have received driving lessons, but I was worried about being unable to pass the test. So, in March, I bought a red Reliant Robin van from Palmers, a motor-cycle, scooter and three-wheeler dealer, whose premises were situated about 100 yards from where my parents lived. Mr. Palmer took me out in the vehicle. He drove round the quiet roads of Worsley Bridge and Copers Cope and then let me loose behind the wheel. I gradually became used to driving it, but it was a very strange feeling at first, only having driven a Lambretta before.

The first family outing that I can remember in the Reliant, was a drive from our home in Borough Green to Hastings. The children travelled in the back of the van, with Alison in her carry-cot. It was a fine day, as I recall and we spent the day at a pleasant park in Hastings. Alison lay in her carry-cot in the sunshine.

In August, we drove down to our hotel in Boscombe in the Reliant. We introduced ourselves to Mr. Fletcher, who showed us to our rooms. We said that we had previously stayed at a hotel in nearby Owls Road the previous year; but had been told that this hotel had closed down. He told us that the owners had gone bankrupt. Apparently they had been very unbusinesslike, supplying guests with all kinds of extras, but forgetting to charge for them. You could never say that Mr. Fletcher was unbusinesslike, as although he was a pleasant chap, he was very efficient. We were however, rather unpopular with him in one respect; our Reliant was not fitted with a suppressor and when we returned to the hotel from an outing, there was interference on the television until I switched off the engine.

We enjoyed our week in Boscombe with the weather staying fine all week. We spent most days on the beach, but we went on one or two outings in the Reliant. I think that the weather was generally good that summer, without being too hot.

The summer of 1972 was one of the most miserable that I can remember. I can only recall one decent weekend during the whole of that summer. We again stayed for a week with Mr. Fletcher. The weather was generally cold and miserable and I was glad that I had the Reliant to take my family out.

1973 produced a much better summer. It was so consistently hot and sunny, that I started to go swimming regularly at Tonbridge Open Air Swimming Baths. I did not know this when I first started to go swimming there, but it was the first year that the pool was heated. One day, I was chatting to one of the attendants, who told me that attendances had been so poor because of the appalling weather of the previous summer, that the Council decided that the pool should be heated.

We went on holiday that year during the first two weeks in September, going to stay in a bungalow at Pevensey Bay, which was owned by one of Brenda's aunts and uncles. Again we travelled down in the Reliant. We had perfect weather during that fortnight and there was a heatwave towards the end of the second week. It was so hot on the journey home and as our route took us through Tonbridge, we decided to stop there and cool off in the swimming pool, before going on to Borough Green. On the second leg of the journey, it was getting unbearably humid. Not long after we arrived home, it started to rain torrentially and suddenly, lightning flashed and thunder roared and what ensued was a storm as equally as spectacular as the one I described in September 1958 earlier in my book. Suddenly, at around 7.30 p.m. the lights went out and did not come on again until very late in the evening.

The summer of 1974 was every bit as miserable as the one in 1972. Brenda had started to take driving lessons in the summer and she hoped to take her test sometime in the autumn and, if successful, intended to buy a new car.

Therefore, we had a cheap holiday that year, stopping just three nights at a hotel in Broadstairs at the beginning of September By this time, the Reliant was becoming, well, 'unreliable', so we decided to travel down to Broadstairs by train. The weather was appalling during our three-day stay and we were glad to get home.

Brenda took her driving test on 1st October and passed first time. On the following Saturday, we went by bus from Borough Green to Dartford, changing at Gravesend. Brenda wanted to buy a new Datsun, so we walked a short distance to a dealers that we knew in Dartford and Brenda bought herself a lovely little gold-coloured car, which she drove home with the children in the back. I cannot now remember how the paperwork was done so quickly, but it was probably arranged beforehand.

I was pleased that we had a decent car at last and I used to put L-plates on the car and drive it from time to time, with Brenda sitting in the passenger seat. However, I still could not pluck up the courage to take a driving test.

We put up the Reliant for sale in a local paper and I cannot recall now how much we asked for it. I think that it was probably a give-away price, as by now it was in rather a decrepit state. On the day that the local paper was due to come out, I went to work as usual and when I returned home, I found that Brenda had been inundated with phone calls. I think that she gave the first caller person who phoned first refusal and as I recall, he accepted the price we were asking.

The summer of 1975 was a very good one. We were to spend a week in a self-catering flat in Weymouth, but unfortunately, misfortune befell David when we stopped for a picnic lunch on the way down. We had stopped on a lovely little clearing at the side of a quiet road in the New Forest. While we were preparing the picnic, David raced off and started to climb a small tree. Suddenly, we heard a thud and saw him lying on the ground. We raced over to him, but he got up and said that he was all right, apart from a slight pain in his arm. However, during the next night, the arm started to become really painful, so the first thing next morning I took him to the Casualty Department at Weymouth Hospital, while Brenda took Alison to the beach. The doctor pronounced that David had suffered a greenstick fracture and the arm was put in plaster. However, he was soon back to his lively self and spent a very enjoyable week at Weymouth in lovely hot weather, spending most of the time on the beach. But, if we thought it had been hot during our holiday of 1975, it was nothing compared to the heat that we were going to experience the following year!

Drought-affected Bough Beech reservoir, Kent, 1976.
By courtesy of Sevenoaks Chronicle.

Chapter Fifteen

THE SUMMER OF 1976 AND THE WINTER OF DISCONTENT

I do not think that anybody who is old enough to remember the summer of 1976 will ever forget it. The heat, almost throughout that summer, from the very beginning to the end of August, was blistering. The reason for these scorching temperatures was that a high-pressure zone from North Africa had drifted north and had remained for a long period over Northern Europe and rain-bearing winds from the west could not penetrate this zone.

Towards the end of June, records were broken for that month, when a record June temperature of 96degF. was recorded at Southampton. On the last Saturday in June, the temperature in London reached 95degF.

By July, which was also a blisteringly hot month, drought conditions existed almost everywhere in the British Isles. There was a ban on hosepipes and sprinklers for watering gardens and a ban on hosepipes for washing cars, The water level in reservoirs was very low and some completely dried up. Vegetables perished in parched fields and consequently, those that were available in the shops were very expensive. Sales of lager and ice cream reached record levels.

By August, the drought situation was so serious that the Government appointed Sports Minister, Denis Howells, to head a team to tackle the problem. He was referred to by the media as 'The Minister for Drought'. It would appear that he possessed some magic, because, just after his appointment, it started to rain at the end of August and by September there were frequent torrential downpours.

I still remember well my own personal experiences that summer. In some ways the summer of 1976 put me in mind of the gorgeous summer of 1959, although '76 was generally much hotter. As in 1959, we had one very wet weekend in June. It would have to have been the weekend that David attended a cub camp on nearby Wrotham Hill (in fact, so nearby, that Brenda and I could see the cubs at camp by looking out of our back bedroom window, which gave us a lovely view of the North Downs. I would estimate the top of Wrotham Hill to be about 4-miles away from where we lived).

I had started a fortnight's holiday on that particular Saturday, the first week which I would spend at home, the second week we were to spend at Weymouth, in the same self-catering flat as in the previous year. At that time David and Alison both went to the same primary school and we had been given permission to take them away for a week.

It had rained nearly all that weekend and it was still raining hard when David and Alison went back to school on the Monday. But, just as in that June weekend in 1959, a boiling hot sun emerged from behind the clouds at around midday. Thereafter, the weather became hotter and hotter that week, until by the Friday it had reached 90degF.

We were due to go on holiday the next day and when we awoke it was even hot then and we felt we were in for an exceptionally hot day. So it turned out with the temperature reaching 95degF. We had put our milk and perishable food, including meat in a cool-box and had put it in the boot of the car. When we arrived at our flat in Weymouth, the milk had gone sour and the meat had gone bad (even in the cool-box). I then had to walk in the blazing heat to the local shop to buy some more provisions. After that, we all took it in turns to have a cool bath. It was hot at night too and although we slept without any bedclothes on top of us, we still found it difficult to sleep.

The temperature in Weymouth the next day reached 93degF. It was at least a mile walk from the flat to the beach and as I was walking through the town, I came over faint and sought shelter in a shop doorway. After a few minutes, I began to feel better and we then continued walking the relatively short distance to the beach. When we arrived there, we all undressed and plunged into the sea and we must have gone into the sea many times that day just to keep cool. We spent our day in roughly the same way the next day, when again, the temperature hovered around the 93deg mark. I think that this was the day that Southampton recorded a record June temperature of 96degF.That evening, we went to a fair in Weymouth, but it was still very hot. I remember one of the fairground men saying that the heat was making him feel ill.

The temperature dropped a degree or two, but it was still boiling hot and we spent most of the days running in and out of the sea and the evenings having cool baths. Usually, on holiday, we used to have some days out in the car, visiting nearby places, such as Dorchester or Bridport, but it was far too hot in the car. We did have to endure the journey back to Kent, however, on the Saturday, but thankfully it was not quite as hot as on the previous Saturday.

When I returned to work on the following Monday, the temperature was still hovering around the 90deg mark. At that time, I worked at the Whitehall branch of the bank and during July, it was so hot, that the Manager allowed us to work without our having to wear jackets and ties.

As mentioned previously in this chapter, the scorching weather continued until the end of August, when it started to rain and by September, there were to be frequent torrential downpours. Unlike 1959, there was to be no Indian summer.

The flat in Weymouth was owned by a Mrs. Wombwell, who was a pleasant lady and we wanted to return there for a week's holiday in 1977. But sadly, just before our holiday, she wrote to us to say that she had fallen ill and we would have to find another flat. We did find another one, which was situated in the centre of the town close to the Weymouth tramway. The weather that week was generally miserable and we particularly noticed this, as we had been spoilt with such good weather the previous two years.

I do not remember much about this holiday, but I do remember sitting on the beach and listening to the Ladies Singles Final at Wimbledon on our portable radio, when our own Virginia Wade beat Betty Stove of Holland. It seemed so appropriate to have a British winner of the Singles title in our Queen's Silver Jubilee year. I remember also seeing a small crowd on the beach awaiting the arrival of a swimmer, who had swum a considerable distance from Jersey.

We had been given an extra day off for the Queen's Silver Jubilee celebrations. The great day was Tuesday 7th June, the day after the Spring Bank Holiday Monday. On the Tuesday, a party was organised for all the local children in King George VIth field in Borough Green. There were sandwiches, jellies and other goodies laid out on trestle tables for the kiddies. The clouds above looked full of rain, but the rain held off while the children were eating, but started to fall during the games, which were held afterwards. It became heavier and when we finally arrived home, we were drenched.

I don't remember any really remarkable weather from the scorching summer of 1976, until the second week of February 1978, when the country was blanketed in snow. The West Country, in particular, suffered, with snow drifts up to 10-feet deep, in places.

I had to go into Sevenoaks hospital for an operation on 7th February. It started to snow heavily just after I arrived there and it was difficult for Brenda to drive 7-miles from Borough Green to visit me, in the icy and treacherous conditions.

Brenda used to be friendly with a girl by the name of Marian, who lived in the adjacent village of Platt. Her daughter was the same age as David and they used to play together. Around the turn of the year, she and her husband Tom had bought a newsagents and general store in Morchard Bishop, a village near Crediton in Devon. They wrote to Brenda in March to say that they had been snowed in the previous month, with snowdrifts of around 10 feet.

Our week's holiday that year was spent in a bungalow at Southbourne, near Bournemouth. The weather was not very good until the Friday, when we had a gorgeous day. We made the most of it by spending the whole day on the beach.

I remember that we had perfect weather during the last three weeks in September that year. I had been sent by the bank on a residential course at their Training Centre at Wimbledon during that time and I had to stay in a hotel in South Kensington and travel each day by coach to Wimbledon. We were allowed to go home at the weekends. The hottest day during that time was the last Thursday (it would have been on the day we had our gruelling 'end of course' tests). I felt particularly sorry for one poor chap who came from Canterbury. In addition to the course tests in the morning and afternoon, he had to take the Practice of Banking examination in the evening, which was considered by most people to be the hardest examination to pass in the Institute of Bankers examinations. These exams were held in the evening and the candidates were almost invariably given the afternoon off. But, the tutors insisted that he completed the course tests in the afternoon, which I thought was most unfair and that he should have been put on a course, which did not clash with the dates of the Institute of Bankers examinations. It was the last night of the course and we celebrated in the bar of the hotel. The IOB exams finished at 9-p.m. and the poor chap turned up to join the celebrations at around 9.30. After a few drinks, he came over quite ill after such a gruelling day.

January 1979 brought in the most severe weather that I could remember since the bitterly cold winter of 1962-63. I remember thinking that these awful winters must run in 16-year-cycles i.e. 1947, 1963 and now 1979.

But, the bad weather was not our only problem in the winter that was known as 'The Winter of Discontent'. Nationally, about a fifth of the workforce was on strike. Amongst other members of the workforce, lorry drivers, oil tanker drivers, railwaymen, dustmen, some hospital workers and even the grave-diggers were on strike. Rubbish piled up in the streets and the dead could not be buried. The last straw for a fed-up public was the return of the Prime Minister, James Callaghan, to an ice-bound and strike-bound Great Britain, smiling and looking tanned and relaxed after a summit meeting in the West Indies.

Not surprisingly, the 'winter of discontent' brought down the Labour Government and its Prime Minister. There was a General Election in May, which the Conservatives won and Margaret Thatcher was elected Prime Minister, the very first woman to attain that position in Great Britain.

My own memories of that winter are still quite vivid. As the trains were not running, I had to catch a coach which left Borough Green bus garage at 6.40-a.m. for Victoria coach station, in order to get to work. As the road gritters were also on strike, the journey was really precarious, with the roads covered in snow and ice. I saw a lot of accidents on these journeys and was thankful that I had arrived at the bank in one piece each day.

Looking forward to our holiday in Sidmouth in 1980.

Chapter Sixteen

ANXIOUS TIMES

We went to Minnis Bay, near Margate, for a week's holiday in 1979. We had rented a ground floor flat and I think that it was, beyond a doubt, the most miserable holiday that we have ever had. The weather was so cold and wet, that I do not remember our going on the beach once during that week. In addition, the people that had rented the flat above were making a din at all hours of the night. We really were glad to get home.

I had a week's holiday in the second week of October and although the weather was lovely throughout that week, on the Friday I received terrible news.

I wanted to go shopping in the afternoon at Maidstone and Brenda said she would collect the children from school and drove me to Borough Green station. I did my shopping in Maidstone and then caught a train from Maidstone station, back to Borough Green. I then set off on the short walk home, but as I was approaching our house, our next door

93

neighbour came out of her house and said, "Go straight away to Brenda's mother's house. Brenda has been taken ill there". At that moment, our doctor drove up in his car, thinking that she had been taken ill at home. However, after I told him that she had been taken ill at her mother's, he told me to jump in the car and we drove the short distance to my mother-in-law's house.

When we arrived, I was extremely shocked to see Brenda lying unconscious on her mother's settee. The doctor pronounced that she had had a stroke. He phoned for an ambulance and I accompanied Brenda to Pembury Hospital. I stayed at the hospital overnight and our next door neighbour very kindly looked after David and Alison.

It was a severe stroke and Brenda was unconscious for eight days, but thanks to her courage and determination, she regained the use of speech and walked again wearing a caliper on the right leg and it was not long before she refused to use her wheelchair. I cannot begin to describe the courage she has shown over the years. The stroke paralysed her right side and very recently, she has started to visit a chiropractor in Bournemouth and amazingly, muscles on Brenda's right side are beginning to come to life after being dormant for over 24 years. I hope and pray that these improvements continue. I will quote the words of my late mother, who often used to say this about Brenda, "She is always cheerful, in spite of everything that has happened and I have never once heard her grumble". The months after Brenda's stroke were an anxious time and no words of mine can adequately express my thanks for the help and support I received from my mother-in-law, my parents, my next-door neighbour and my employers. David and Alison were also very helpful and supportive. What happened to Brenda must been a terrible blow to them.

One thing that I did not want was for Brenda to be stuck in the 'four walls' for too long. So, I really had to overcome my fear of taking a driving test and I commenced taking driving lessons on 29th February with a local instructor. I think that I had had three lessons, when I was advised that he had died of a heart-attack while out shopping with his wife (I trust that this was nothing to do with my driving!).

I had to find another driving instructor in a hurry, so I went to the British School of Motoring in Maidstone and enrolled. My instructor suggested that I put in for my driving test straight away and I received a rapid reply to my application. My test was to be at 11 a.m. on Monday 12th May. It was already the end of March and my instructor suggested that I have two evening lessons after work and one at the weekend. Luckily, my instructor was very thorough. I remember the weather being lovely at the beginning of May and I recall doing my 'reverses' and 'three-point turns' in quiet streets, lined each side with trees bearing gorgeous pink blossom.

All too soon, the great day arrived. At the end of my last lesson, I said to my instructor, "What time shall I report to you on Monday?".

"Nine-o'clock", he replied.

"Nine-o'clock?", I said, "But my test is not until 11!".

"Knowing your temperament, you are going to need two hours to unwind before your test", he replied.

Even two hours of driving before the test, did not really steady my nerves, because, when the examiner asked me to drive off, my legs went completely numb immediately after I had turned right out of the Test Centre. I was in a panic! I could scarcely feel the accelerator. I thought "I will have to ask the Examiner to use the dual-control brake and then I will fail my test". But, someone was smiling on me, it was quite a long stretch of road, with no hazards and by the time I had come to a roundabout, the use of my legs magically returned. The examiner then asked me to turn right at the roundabout. After that, I felt more relaxed and things seemed to go smoothly.

Talking of miracles, a very strange thing happened to me that day and on the day before. This was a Sunday and I was relaxing in gorgeous weather in the garden with my father. Suddenly, a bird flew over us and left his calling card on my shoulder. The following day, of course, was the day of my test. Again, it was a beautiful day. My driving instructor took pity on me during my two-hour stint and suggested that we pull over for a 10-minute break. I tried to relax by resting my elbow on the open window, then, lo and behold, another bird flew over and left his calling card on my elbow. Now this had neither happened to me before and nor has it happened since. Being visited in this way by a bird is meant to bring you luck and it did.

I finally arrived back at the Test Centre. The examiner asked me some questions on the Highway Code and then said, "You have passed your test". I am ashamed to say that I burst into tears. So much had depended on my passing the test. I could now take my wife and children anywhere that I wanted. I could see why my instructor insisted on driving back to the BSM centre.

I immediately phoned Brenda from a telephone box in Maidstone Post Office, to tell her the news and then walked to Maidstone East station to catch a train back to Borough Green. It was a beautiful afternoon and we relaxed in the front garden until around 6-o'clock. I then thought that I should take the car out for a spin. I had heard of one or two people passing their tests and not having the confidence to get behind the wheel shortly afterwards and then losing the confidence to drive altogether. I did not want to be among that number. Although I had driven alone in the Reliant van countless times, it still felt strange and I was glad to get home in one piece, even though I had only driven to the nearby village of Shipbourne and back. The next day, when I had shaken off the euphoria of passing my test, I went out and drove with confidence.

Unfortunately, the glorious early May weather did not last and the second half of the month saw the start of the wettest and most miserable spell of late spring and summer weather that I can remember. After the glorious weather in early May, we did not have another spell of decent weather until the last few days of July. I remember ringing my brother Geoff, who was working in Brussels at that time and moaning about the almost incessant rain. "You're lucky", he said, "It has been twice as bad in Belgium".

I was lucky enough to have a week's holiday at the very end of July and I felt run-down by the time my holiday came round. The weather was glorious that week and my mother-in-law insisted that I got out, while she looked after Brenda some afternoons. It was very good of her and I was able to go to the Open Air Lido at Tonbridge. That week off in such glorious weather really pulled me round and I returned to work feeling refreshed.

Feeling much better, I really began to look forward to our family holiday in another two weeks time. We were to spend a week at a hotel in Sidmouth and then two days at a guesthouse in Lyme Regis over the August Bank Holiday weekend. We were to holiday in Sidmouth for a further four consecutive years.

In spite of Brenda having had a stroke, these family holidays were the happiest ones that I have known.

Mount Pleasant Hotel, Sidmouth.

Chapter Seventeen

FAMILY HOLIDAYS AT SIDMOUTH

Once I had returned to work, the weather became as bad again as it had been in June and most of July. We were due to travel down to Sidmouth in a fortnight's time and I viewed the situation with apprehension, 'Where would we go and what would we do, if it rains all the time?', I thought.

Our holiday started on Saturday 17th August and on that morning, we miraculously awoke to beautiful weather. We had perfect weather at Sidmouth and then we stayed at Lyme Regis for a further two days over the August Bank Holiday and again, we had perfect weather. We had fantastic luck with our holidays at Sidmouth and in all, we stayed there for five consecutive years. The weather in 1980, 1981, 1983 and 1984 was not only good, but perfect. 1982 was the only year that we had miserable weather. Amazingly enough, 1980 and 1981 were generally poor summers, although 1983 and 1984 were good ones.

We stayed at the Canterbury Hotel, which was situated near The Byes, which was a lovely stretch of parkland, running alongside the River Sid. We liked Sidmouth very much, as the beach was ideal for children and the weather was so good, that we spent most of the week there. We left the hotel on the Saturday, but the weather was so good that we decided to stay on holiday over the August Bank Holiday weekend. We fancied spending it in Lyme Regis. I liked Lyme had many happy memories of the place, as I had spent two Scout Summer Camps at nearby Charmouth in 1949 and 1950.

We came across a guesthouse, which had vacancies and we booked in for two nights. The children loved the beach and David spent most of his time searching for crabs in the rock pools near the Cobb, a short stone pier made famous in the film 'The French Lieutenant's Woman'. David used to race up the beach to show Brenda and I what he had caught.

In February 1981, the bank gave me a compassionate posting to their Sevenoaks branch. Although Brenda was a lot better, it was comforting to know that it would not take me long to get home in the case of an emergency. The manager of the Whitehall branch had been very good to me and had allowed me to have time off when I had needed it. I enjoyed working at Sevenoaks branch and there also, the manager was very good to me.

In August, we splashed out on a fortnight's holiday at Sidmouth, but this time we wanted to stay at a larger hotel. We liked the look of the Mount Pleasant Hotel, which was situated in quite an imposing position on the other side of the River Sid, and overlooking it. So we wrote to the proprietors and booked up for a fortnight. It was a lovely hotel with a nine-hole putting green on the front lawn. The food was excellent and the rooms were very comfortable. We spent an enjoyable fortnight in perfect weather. We were very lucky, as most of my colleagues at work had had miserable weather.

We spent some days on the beach at Sidmouth and others at either Lyme Regis or Budleigh Salterton. David liked both these resorts, as there were plenty of rock pools. On the middle Sunday, we travelled to a village called Morchard Bishop, near Crediton, where we spent a lovely day with Brenda's friends - Marion and Tom. They were telling us about the bad time they had in February 1978, when the snow was 10-feet deep in places. In the afternoon, I went with Tom to see a village cricket match, the cricket field being on high ground, with beautiful views of

Dartmoor on one side and Exmoor on the other.

We were glad that we had been fortified by a fortnight's great weather in August, as that year we had the worst December weather that I can remember. It started at the beginning of the month and there was so much snow and ice, that I was unable to use the car three times to go to work and had to walk to the bus garage to catch a bus to Sevenoaks. We lived on quite a steep hill and when I drove out of the garage, I had to turn left down a steep slope and then turn sharply right up a steep slope.

The snow was so thick and the ice underneath so treacherous, that the car could not get up it, so I returned the car to the garage and walked to the village to catch a bus. It snowed heavily nearly every day that month and as most of the staff kept their cars on a piece of waste ground at the back of the branch, most of us brought shovels so that we could dig ourselves out at night.

The last day that I had to catch a bus to work that December was on Christmas Eve. It had snowed very heavily the night before and it was so bad in the morning, that I did not attempt to take the car out, but walked straight down to the bus garage to catch a bus. In those days, the banks used to close at 12 noon on Christmas Eve and we then used to have drinks in the office with the manager before going home. I had to make my way to Sevenoaks bus station, but first I had to call at an off-licence to buy a bottle of whisky for our doctor who had been so good to Brenda since her stroke.

I got off the bus at the crossroad in Borough Green and then walked down an icy steep pavement to the surgery. It was a wonder that the doctor got his bottle of whisky, as I almost slipped over several times on the icy pavement. I wondered whether, in fact, the doctor would be there in the early afternoon on Christmas Eve, but there was a little party going on in the waiting room, so I was able to give the bottle to him personally.

I cannot now recall whether snow actually fell on Christmas Day, but it was so miserable with snow, ice and slush. I remember taking Brenda, her mother and the children to Orpington the day after Boxing Day, which was a Sunday, to spend the day with Brenda's youngest sister and her husband. The roads were still treacherous, with plenty of frozen slush about.

There was plenty of snow about at the beginning of January and I remember Tuesday 7th January being a particularly bad day. Again, I had to leave the car in the garage and take the bus to work. One chap who lived in the Medway towns could not get to work at all, as snow had blocked the A229 on Bluebell Hill, as it had all other routes out of the Medway towns. However, I *do* recall that February was a much better month, weatherwise.

July 1982 was a hot and sunny month, but an anxious month for me. Brenda had been taken ill and had spent all month in Sevenoaks Hospital. We were due to go to Sidmouth again for a week's holiday in the middle of August and once Brenda was home, I asked the doctor if we should still go? "I don't see why not, but Brenda will have to take it easy", he said. She did not feel very well on this holiday and what with the miserable weather, I was not sorry to get home. I think that the children enjoyed themselves though. Brenda bravely insisted that we went to Lyme Regis twice, as the children enjoyed the beach so much there.

Although we went to the same hotel in 1983, we were slightly apprehensive about going there, as the ownership had changed hands. But, we needn't have worried, because the new proprietors looked after us just as well as the old ones had done. We had a lovely week's holiday in glorious weather. We visited our usual haunts, such as Lyme Regis and Budleigh Salterton, but one day, by way of a change, we took the children to Farway Country Park, so that they could go riding, which they both liked. I won't bore the reader by being too repetitive about our holidays at Sidmouth, as mostly we tended to visit the same places and do the same things. We had a lovely week's holiday in perfect weather again in 1984. The thing that I remember most about this holiday was the journey home.

David was aged 17 in March of that year and had passed his driving test in May. As we were about to leave the hotel, he said to me, "May I drive home, Dad?".

I thought about it for a few moments and then said, "Why not". Even at this early age he was a good driver. A policeman had been following him through the narrow lanes around Plaxtol and Ightham and had pulled him over and said, "You were going slightly too fast. You are an excellent driver, but you just need to watch your speed a little". So, we set off and David drove steadily, until we reached the Cadnam area of Hampshire, where the A31 joins the M27. But, once on the motorway, he really put his foot down. We passed Rownhams service station and then, instead of forking left up the M3, carried on up the M27 towards Portsmouth and during the whole time that we were on the M 27, he was only overtaken once, by an Aston Martin! He then drove up the A3 to Guildford, then took the A25 which took us to a stone's-throw of our home.

I cannot think of any remarkable weather in 1985 and the summer was rather miserable, as I recall. At the end of the year, we were getting ready to move home.

On 13th January 1986, we moved from our semi-detached property in

Borough Green, to a lovely linked-detached house in Leybourne, near West Mailing. The weather was exceptionally mild for that time of the year and we moved without difficulty. We had wanted this lovely house so much, that I took a heck of a risk and took out a bridging loan, as we had not completed on the sale of the Borough Green property, nor had we exchanged contracts.

In contrast to January, February was a bitterly cold month and so was the first week in March. I did, however receive some good news towards the end of February. Contracts had been exchanged on our old house, with completion set for 10th March. March 1st, however, however, was a bitterly cold day and the pipes froze in the empty property. Two or three days after that, there was a thaw and the pipes burst, flooding the property. Our buyer had prudently insured against fire and flood on exchanging contracts, but as my policy was still in force, I said that I would deal with the matter. As far as I can remember, everything was right by the completion date.

My parents came to see our new house in April, together with my brother Geoff and his wife, Janet. Dad had not been well for some time, but my mother and my brother had persuaded him to come. Dad looked fairly well and was in good spirits and we all spent a pleasant day together. But, just after he arrived home, he became very ill and sadly died on 15th May. He had been a splendid Dad and I cannot remember a warmer welcoming smile when he used to open the door to Brenda and I when we went to visit my parents. We then received an equally welcoming smile from my mother, who was usually preparing the dinner. I will never forget the long chats Dad and I used to have while sitting on chairs in the back garden on warm Sunday afternoons. I missed him very much.

We did not take a holiday that summer, as we were still counting the cost of moving in the previous January. However, we knew that Mum was obviously feeling down after the death of Dad, so we promised that we would take her to the lovely Mount Pleasant Hotel in Sidmouth the following year.

After the very cold spell in February and at the beginning of March, the weather for the rest of the year was unremarkable, although the summer was rather miserable. But, the following year was to throw everything at us (apart from a heatwave!).

The Vine, Sevenoaks, showing seven oaks with only one remaining standing.
By courtesy of Sevenoaks Chronicle.

Chapter Eighteen

HEAVY SNOW, HOUSE STRUCK BY LIGHTNING AND HURRICANE

On Sunday 11th January 1987, I went for a walk in Manor Park, West Malling. When I got out of the car and started walking, I noticed how bitterly cold was the wind. I had not felt so cold since Boxing Day 1962, which heralded the start of the bitterly cold winter of 1962-63. I did not walk for long and when I arrived back at the car, I thought to myself, 'We are in for some snow'. The following night, it started to snow very heavily and it was still snowing furiously the next morning. The snow was at least 3-feet deep and deeper where it had drifted. It would have been quite impossible to drive the car out of the garage, let alone out of the estate. It would have been impossible to walk out of the estate to the main road, as there were very deep snowdrifts in places. Therefore, I rang up the bank and told them it was impossible to get in. The rules of the bank in such a case are that you must report to the nearest branch, if that is possible. Now, my nearest branch was at Larkfield, a distance of about 1 1/2 miles from where I lived. But, that was out of the question also, because it would have been dangerous to walk out of the estate. I did not like having to admit to the bank that I could not attend work, as I have always taken a pride in succeeding in getting to school or work in bad weather. In fact, in February 1991, the Chief Clerk told me off for attempting to get in to work in very bad conditions and told me to return home immediately. I had only failed to get in once before and that was on the day after the severe floods in Kent, when I worked at the bank's Sloane Street branch.

It continued to snow and snow that morning and showed no signs of stopping, so I put on my Wellingtons and waded with difficulty through the snow to the General Stores on the estate. Fortunately, it was only a short walk, but when I arrived there, I was shocked. I saw that the shelves were practically empty, as if a swarm of locusts had devoured everything. Fortunately, I managed to get some milk and one or two other items to keep us going for the rest of the day.

When I left the shop, I looked into the distance and all I could see was an apparently endless snowy wilderness. Then a chilling thought struck me, 'What if the snow goes on and on and lorries can't get through to deliver food to the shops? There was hardly anything left in the shop now and it is only ten-o'clock in the morning. We could starve'. I then realised just how much I had taken such simple things, such as 'food and drink on the table' for granted.

It continued to snow for the rest of the day, that night and it was still snowing the next morning. Again, it was completely out of the question to get to work or even to the local branch. Now, the assistant manager's secretary also lived on the estate and we used to take it in turns to use our cars. Now, she was one of the most efficient and conscientious people that I have come across and she agreed that it was impossible to get to work. I walked again to the local shop early that morning, in the forlorn hope of being able to buy some milk and food, but by some miracle a delivery lorry had managed to get through.

At last, it stopped snowing that day and when I woke up, I noticed that conditions had slightly improved. So, I rang my colleague from work and we both agreed that it would still be impossible to get to Sevenoaks, but that we should make the effort to walk to the Larkfield branch. I rang the branch at 9-a.m., but they told me that they had enough staff, as staff who lived in the village had been reporting for work. My colleague received the same answer. As I intended to walk to Larkfield anyway, I said to Brenda that I might as well walk to the Safeways supermarket in the village to stock up on provisions. I also wanted to buy my mother a birthday card, as it was her birthday on the coming Sunday. Ever since I was small, I never failed to give or send my mother a card and a present. The present could wait until we were able to visit her, but I wanted her to get the card on time. I, therefore, bought a card and sent it to her that morning.

The following morning, I rang my colleague early. The weather had improved further and there had been no more snow, but the conditions were far from good. We both agreed that we must make the attempt to get to Sevenoaks. We travelled in her car, and although the roads were still dangerous, we arrived at work in one piece. After that conditions began to improve rapidly, but I think that there was some flooding, due to the vast amount of melting snow.

In August, we took Mum, as promised, to the Mount Pleasant Hotel in Sidmouth. Sadly, the children were now too old to want to come with us and unfortunately, we did not get the perfect weather that we had experienced previously, apart from 1982, but it wasn't too bad.

I can only really remember two events in connection with this holiday after all this time. My cousin David and his wife Rosemary, who lived in the village of Upottery, near Honiton, invited us to lunch in the town on the Sunday. After an excellent lunch, we drove back to their home, where we spent an enjoyable afternoon and Rosemary gave us a lovely tea.

My second memory is with regard to a game of tennis with Mum one evening on a public tennis court in Sidmouth. I had not played Mum at tennis since the 1950s and had never beaten her, which is, perhaps, not surprising, as she had won the Ladies Singles Cup 17 consecutive times at her club and had won the LCC Ladies Doubles Cup at Queens Club with her partner Iris in 1953 and they had been runners-up in 1956 and 1963. Mum was now 76 years of age and she still beat me. Sadly, we never played tennis again, because during the following year, she had an accident, which stopped her from playing.

We had not been back long from our holiday, when our house was struck by lightning. On Friday 21st August, we went to bed at about 10-p.m. We had not been in bed long, when we saw forked lightning and heard rumbles of thunder. Soon, the lightning was getting closer and closer and the thunder louder and louder. Suddenly, there was an almighty bang and the lights went out. Fortunately, I had a torch by the side of my bed, which was fortunate as Brenda, needed to see to put on her boots and caliper and then we needed to see in order to get downstairs. I feared that there might have been structural damage to the house, so I picked up my torch and went out into the front garden. By this time, it was raining torrentially. It was quite a powerful beam that I shone on the roof but I could see no damage. We sat downstairs for about two hours, by which time the storm had abated. We then climbed the stairs, aided by the beam from the torch and went to bed. Brenda insisted on keeping on her boots and caliper in case the thunder and lightning returned. This was, of course, a sensible precaution, but it must have been uncomfortable for her. We managed to get some sleep and we were not disturbed by more thunder and lightning.

We got up quite early next morning, as we were worried about any possible damage to the house. Fortunately, it still gets light quite early in August and we were able to get ourselves some breakfast. Our son, David arrived home just after that. He had been staying with friends overnight. I think that Alison must have been staying with friends over the weekend, as she was not home at the time. I asked David if he would mind taking a look in the loft; I could have done so myself, but we had no loft ladder and David, at his age, was obviously more agile than I was. So, David shinned up into the loft and I went out into the garden to see if I could see any damage to the roof. What I saw next absolutely amazed me. David's fingers suddenly appeared through the roof, reminiscent of the fingers of Orson Welles sticking up out of a drain-cover in Vienna in the film 'The Third Man'. He then came downstairs, bringing with him pieces of molten ridge tile, which had fallen into the water-tank. Somebody really was looking after us that night, as the house could have easily caught fire. He then drove down to B&Q in Larkfield to get some fuse wire. We soon had our lights on again, but we discovered that the lightning strike had put our fridge, freezer and telephone out of action, but amazingly enough the television was all right. This was, I think, because the lightning struck the end of the house where the fridge freezer and telephone were and the television was at the other end of the house. We then went out into the back garden and round to the side of the house, which had been struck by the lightning. We saw that there was some damage to the brickwork and we later learned that a bolt of lightning had struck Leybourne Church and had travelled horizontally across a field and then struck our house and that of our next-door neighbours. Their house did not suffer as much damage as ours, although my neighbour told me that his telephone had been put out of action, together with another piece of electrical apparatus, but I cannot now recall what it was. I had all the damage put right, which was fortunately covered by my insurance policy.

When I returned to work on the Monday, I took a piece of molten ridge-tile to show my friends at work and to tell them what had happened.

I took the rest of my annual leave on 14th, 15th and 16th October. The 15th was a Thursday and it had been raining very hard in the afternoon and in the evening, the air became very still. Stormy weather was predicted at the beginning of the week when the Meteorological Office identified a depression strengthening over the Atlantic. Later that evening, we listened to the weather forecast and Michael Fish said "Earlier on today a lady rang the BBC and said she heard that there was a hurricane on the way. Well don't worry if you are watching, there isn't". The next day Britain awoke to a trail of devastation wreaked by the worst storm in 300 years.

We went to bed at around 10.30-p.m. and I was soon asleep, but I was awoken at around 4-a.m. by the most ferocious, howling wind that I have ever heard. I looked out of the window and saw frequent showers of sparks, caused presumably, by falling trees hitting power cables. The storm seemed to be even more fierce by 5.30-a.m. and I heard later that a wind velocity of 94-mph had been recorded in London and more than 100- mph on the South Coast. Our lights went out about that time and again, I was glad that I had a torch handy.

The storm had abated somewhat by the time that it became light and I went out into the front and then the back garden to see what damage the hurricane had caused. But, the fates had been kind to us. Apart from a circular clothes-line that had been blown inside-out, there was no other damage. Perhaps, it had been decreed that we had suffered enough as a result of the lightning strike.

I was glad that I was on leave and that I did not have to struggle in to work that Friday. I probably would not have been able to get to Sevenoaks anyway, as the roads were littered with falling trees. It was bad enough trying to get in on the following Monday. I drove out of Borough Green and as far as the roundabout near Ightham. I had been told that there was one route open through the country lanes to Sevenoaks, the A25 still having been blocked by falling trees, but the policeman on the roundabout advised me that a lorry driver had tried to use the country lane route and his lorry had become stuck in a narrow lane, thus closing this route to traffic. So, I had to drive to the nearby

M20, then get onto the M25 Motorway at Swanley and then take the turning off to Sevenoaks. The traffic was very heavy and I was considerably late for work.

The hurricane had caused immense damage, some 15 million trees being felled and whole forests decimated. Buildings suffered severe damage and many had their roofs ripped off and hundreds of roads and railway lines were blocked by fallen trees. Along the South Coast, damage to yachts and boatyards was extensive and many boats were driven ashore. At Folkestone, a Sea Link ferry was blown aground and its crew had to be rescued. However, I was sad to hear that the pier at Shanklin had been completely destroyed by the storm. I had been to Shanklin twice and in July 1954 had sat on the pier listening to a commentary of the Men's Singles Final at Wimbledon, when Jaroslav Drobny defeated Ken Rosewall.

There was a lot of damage in and around Sevenoaks, the hurricane destroying six of the famous 'Seven Oaks' which bordered the town's cricket ground.

16 people had been killed as a result of the hurricane, many of them by falling trees and debris. *All in all I was glad to see the back of 1987.*

Bournemouth beach.

Chapter Nineteen

WEATHER 1988-91

The summer of 1988 was generally miserable. There was only one weekend when it was good enough to sunbathe in the garden and that was at the beginning of August. Later that month, I drove down to Cornwall with Brenda and her mother. We were staying at a hotel in Falmouth and Brenda's mother was going to stay a week with her youngest daughter and her husband, who now lived at Helford.

Travelling down to Cornwall on a Saturday in the school holidays could be a nightmare; there were almost invariably bottlenecks on the Exeter By-pass, Okehampton and Launceston. Therefore, I planned to drive across Dartmoor once I reached Devon, but, to my dismay, when I arrived there, most of the county was blanketed in fog. So I decided, then and there, not to drive across Dartmoor. The first bottleneck occurred, as expected, on the Exeter By-pass. We were not much further on than Honiton. I felt so frustated, what with the fog and the traffic-jam. The fog had cleared slightly and as we were crawling along, I noticed one or two vehicles turning left up a farm track. However, they seemed to be driving past the farmhouse. 'I wonder whether one can get on to another road?', I thought to myself. Now, I will try anything rather than fume in a traffic-jam, so I also drove up this farm-track. I was lucky, because I succeeded in getting on to a road, south of the Exeter By-pass. But, by this time, the fog was so thick that I lost my way and found myself on the outskirts of Sidmouth. I then took the road from Sidmouth to Exeter, which I knew well, having used it several times during our many holidays in the resort. It was very foggy around Sidmouth, but cleared once I was on the road to Exeter. I then took the A30 to Okehampton. There was a bad traffic-jam there as the by-pass had not been built at that time. A similar situation occurred at Launceston in Cornwall. We had arranged to meet Brenda's sister and her husband at a lay-by near Falmouth, eventually arriving there over two hours late. Brenda's mother then went off with them to Helford and I then drove to our hotel in Falmouth.

The next day I awoke with a bad headache. It had been a long drive from Kent to Cornwall and I had had thick fog and bad traffic jams to contend with. So, I drove to nearby Pendennis Castle in Falmouth and sat in the car in the castle grounds, which overlooked the sea. I found this very restful and by lunch time my headache had gone. The next day, I drove out to The Lizard, which I think is the most southerly point in the British Isles. The day after that, I drove to Helford and we spent an enjoyable day with Brenda's sister and husband and Brenda's mother. They had a lovely bungalow and a beautiful garden, from which you had magnificent views of the Helford River. I cannot now remember what we got up to on the Wednesday and Thursday. The weather that week had been generally miserable, but on the Friday, we had a lovely day, which we made the most of by spending it on the beach.

We took Brenda's mother home, after Brenda's sister and husband brought her over to our hotel early on the Saturday morning. I was determined to go back via Dartmoor after the trials and tribulations of our journey down and I set out towards Plymouth travelling through Truro, St. Austell and Liskeard, I arrived at the roundabout just before the Tamar Bridge and saw a long queue of traffic. So, I turned left at the roundabout towards Callington and then drove over Dartmoor. I did not have any problems with traffic on the journey home.

We had a very good late spring and summer in 1989. The marvellous weather started on 1st May, and it was the most sweltering May I have known, apart from 1976. I was still working in the Securities Department at the Sevenoaks branch of the bank and as the volume of business was expanding so much, additional premises were needed. So, in March, the Management, Loans Department and most of the Securities Department moved into new premises a few doors away. Three members of the latter department had to remain in the old building: a chap who was slightly older than me, a young girl and myself. We felt very envious, because the new office had air-conditioning. We were not too worried about it at first, because at the end of March and April, the weather was cold and miserable, but when May arrived with its exceptional heat, we found ourselves sweltering in our somewhat cramped office. So, we complained to the management, who promised to have air-conditioning installed as soon as possible. We did not get it until the end of June, after we had sweltered for nearly two months, but July was a hot month as well, so we appreciated it then.

We wanted to take Mum on holiday again, so we had a discussion about it at the beginning of the year, deciding that we would like to go to Bournemouth. So, I sent off for a brochure and when I received it, Brenda and I drove to Mum's house. We pored over the brochure and made a short list of about six likely hotels. We could not make up our minds as to which one would be best, so we literally picked out one with a pin. It was the Woodford Court Hotel in the Alum Chine area of Bournemouth. I wrote to them, asking if they had two rooms vacant for the week commencing with the Spring Bank Holiday and they wrote back, advising us that they had these vacancies and we duly booked. We found the proprietors to be very friendly and nothing was too much trouble for them. The beds were comfortable and the food excellent. Brenda and I liked the place so much, that we returned every single Spring Bank Holiday week up to and including 2001. Michael and Angela, the proprietors, retired the following October and the hotel was sold.

Returning now to our holiday in 1989; I drove to Sydenham to pick up Mum and then I set out for Bournemouth. It was a hot day and I was glad when we arrived at our hotel. The next day was just as hot and we spent the morning on the beach.

In the afternoon, I took Mum and Brenda to see Piddlehinton Camp, near Dorchester, where I had been stationed during my National Service. Mum had never seen the Camp, although she and Dad had seen the Training Centre at Devizes when they came to see my Passing Out Parade. The Camp was now empty and looked derelict and forlorn. I showed Mum some of the old huts, which were still standing and then we went to Dorchester. It was boiling hot the next day, which was the Bank Holiday Monday. We spent the morning on the beach and as it was so hot, it was probably sensible to spend just the morning on the beach and in the afternoon, I drove to the New Forest.

The weather was still very hot on the Tuesday and the Wednesday, but I cannot now remember what we did on those two days. This spell of very hot weather ended in a storm the next day. We had decided to go to Dorchester again in the afternoon and for old time's sake, I wanted to have tea and cakes in the Old Tea House, Mum and Brenda being agreeable. I had not set foot in the place since September 1952, when I first had to report to Piddlehinton Camp and I gone in to have a cup of tea before catching a bus to the camp.

When we left the Tea House, we noticed that the sky was becoming dark and menacing. Fortunately, we did not have a long walk to our car, but just after I drove off, the storm hit us. Thunder roared and lightning flashed and it started to rain in torrents. Some of the roads were beginning to flood and I was worried about not being able to get back to our hotel. Flooding in the Canford Heath area was particularly bad, but we arrived at the hotel in one piece. The next day was a dry day, but it was cold and miserable and the next day I drove to Mum's house, having had a very good holiday. Both July and August were hot months and all in all we had had a very good summer.

On 25th January 1990, we were struck by another hurricane. It was the second day of a two-day 'customer relations course' that I was attending at the bank's Local Head Office in Maidstone and the wind was getting up in the early morning, when I was driving from Leybourne to Maidstone along the M20. I parked my car, as I had the previous day in the car park at Maidstone East station and I then walked the short distance to LHO. The force of the wind increased during the morning and by lunchtime, it had reached gale-force. At 1 p.m., I walked with difficulty to the car park to eat my sandwiches in the car and by this time, the wind was blowing with such a force that it was rocking the car up and down. I looked across to the other side of the station and saw tiles cascading down from the roof of a pub. I lost no time in getting back, as the pub was almost adjacent to our LHO.

We sat down in the classroom for our afternoon lectures and our lecturer had just started to speak, when the door opened and two policemen entered. They said that all non-essential personnel should go home straightaway. We were hardly essential personnel, as we were on a course, so we packed up immediately and made for our homes. The policemen warned us not to use the M20, as the gale-force winds had blown over some high-sided lorries. So, I decided to go home via Aylesford, thus avoiding the motorway.

I switched on the radio, to hear that Gordon Kaye (Rene in the television programme 'Allo, Allo') had been injured, when a branch of a tree had crashed through his windscreen. Therefore, I was very nervous when I was driving through the wooded areas around Aylesford, as there were branches of trees on the road and some smaller branches were flying about. Thankfully, I managed to get home in one piece. Strangely enough, this mini-hurricane did more damage to our property than had the hurricane of October 1987. Then, the only damage we suffered was the wreckage of our circular clothes-line, but this time, we lost a lot of tiles from the roof and some fence panels had been blown down.

On 9th June, we were to receive bad news. Brenda's brother rang up to say that their mother had had a stroke and an ambulance had taken her to Maidstone hospital. We raced over to the hospital and were shocked to see that Brenda's mother was unconscious. Sadly, she never regained consciousness and died on 3rd August. She had been in hospital over seven weeks; she had been in Maidstone Hospital for about a month and then was transferred to Linton Hospital, where she died. My mother-in-law was a lovely lady and had been a tower of strength to us all.

Although the weather was the last thing on our mind at such a time, I could not help noticing how generally miserable the weather was when my mother-in-law was in Maidstone Hospital and how blazing hot it was when we used to visit her in Linton Hospital. In fact, the day that she died, the then highest temperature in the British Isles of over 98degF, was recorded in Worcestershire.

As far as I can remember, the blazing hot weather continued through most of August.

I cannot really remember much remarkable weather in 1991, except for a few days of very bad weather in the second week of February. The summer was, as I recall, good without being generally anything like as hot as those of the previous two years.

On Thursday 7th February, it had snowed heavily and when I woke up the next morning there were several inches of snow on the ground and everywhere looked like a snowy white wilderness. The conditions were very bad, but I decided to make an attempt to get to work. Driving over to Sevenoaks, the conditions were really awful and when I arrived at the Buckhurst car park, Sevenoaks, there were hardly any cars in the snowbound car park. Usually, by the time I arrive, the car park was nearly full so something told me that I should not have attempted this journey.

I struggled along the narrow alleyway from the car park to the bank and rang the doorbell. The Manager's Assistant answered it and said, "Why did you attempt to come to work on a morning like this? Go home straight away". 'There's gratitude!', I thought, but I realised that he was right, I shouldn't have attempted to come in on such a morning.

If I thought that the journey to work had been difficult, the journey home was worse. The, roads were like an ice-rink, but I managed to get to Borough Green. There an accident had completely blocked the Maidstone Road, but I thought that I would be able to get through the village by going up Western Road, then turning right into the High Street, before rejoining the Maidstone road. I was about to turn right into the High Street, when I saw that it too was blocked by an accident. I started to feel panicky. There was only one other feasible route home and that was to drive towards Wrotham and then on to the A20. It would have been disastrous to have attempted to get home through the country lanes. Thankfully, I just about managed to get home.

Brenda then said, "Can you and David go straight away to Tesco's in Larkfield to get in plenty of provisions?".

"Use my car, Dad", said David, "Your light car will never stay on the road in these conditions". At that time, David owned a large Rover and we managed to get to Tesco's, stock up on food and drink and get home again in one piece! The terrible weather lasted over the weekend, but mercifully it began to improve on the Monday.

As mentioned, the summer of 1991 was generally good, but not as good as the ones of 1989 and 1990. I retired from the bank on 31st December 1991 and will conclude my book, as at that date, as I can only think of four instances of really extraordinary weather from that date until the present day and do not have any particular personal memories in their regard.

These four recollections are the summer of 1995, which rivalled 1976 with its ferocious heat; the serious flooding in October 2000; the exceptionally hot weather of 2003, when on Sunday 10th August, a record temperature of 101.3degF was recorded at Faversham in Kent and the terrible floods at Boscastle in Cornwall in August 2004, which were so reminiscent of the Lynmouth floods in 1952, but fortunately, unlike in the Lynmouth disaster, no one was killed.

I daresay that I have forgotten some remarkable weather which occurred over the years, particularly over the last twelve years or so, as I have often heard it said that one can usually remember events which took place a long time ago more clearly than more recent events. I hope that the reader will forgive any such omissions.